WHAT YOUR COLLEAGUES ARE SAYING

As a teacher of 28 years this is the book I've been waiting for . . . It weaves together the threads of mindfulness and executive function through brain-based research and science. It offers us practical strategies and techniques that can help our students to feel safe, increase self-regulation skills, and become more resilient. This is a MUST READ for all teachers and administrators!

—Trish Burton,
Third Grade Teacher

Gravity Goldberg reminds us that our schools must be supportive of our students in their entirety—their brains and bodies. With practical recommendations to improve students' regulatory skills, mental health, and focus, this book empowers teachers and school leaders with tools to improve students' communication, collaboration, and comprehension.

—Molly Ness,
author, teacher educator

In *The Body-Brain Connection: Evidence-Based Ways to Reduce Anxiety, Boost Engagement, and Increase Comprehension Across Classrooms*, Gravity Goldberg offers a transformative approach to teaching that honors both students' humanity and the educator's role in fostering connection. By emphasizing safety, embodied learning, and productive struggle, Goldberg provides actionable strategies and reflection practices to reduce anxiety, boost engagement, and build a supportive community. This book is an essential guide for educators seeking to create grounded and impactful learning experiences that nurture both the mind and the body.

—Afrika Afeni Mills,
founder and CEO of Continental Drift LLC,and author of *Open Windows, Open Minds: Developing Antiracist, Pro-Human Students*

Traditionally, the role of teachers has been to help students develop their minds. Gravity Goldberg helps us understand that learning actually happens in a synergy between our minds *and* our bodies and offers teachers a wealth of practical strategies for supporting this connection in their day-to-day teaching, whatever grade and subject they teach.

—Carl Anderson,
educator, and author of *Teaching Fantasy Writing: Lessons That Inspire Student Engagement and Creativity K–6*

Do you have stressed and anxious students? Students who are disengaged and not understanding lessons? If this sounds like some of the students in your classroom, Gravity Goldberg's newest book is for you. It offers compelling evidence and advice for creating a learning environment in which students are supported to engage.

—Douglas Fisher,
Best-selling author, Professor and Chair of Educational Leadership, San Diego State University

The Body-Brain Connection

"Feeling is revolutionary, a disruption of the status quo. Though it feels personal and happens in our bodies, it doesn't need to be a solitary action. Feeling and connection bring us into the world and into relationship with one another."

— Prentis Hemphill, *What It Takes to Heal: How Transforming Ourselves Can Change the World*

"Despite the well-documented effects of anger, fear, and anxiety on the ability to reason, many programs continue to ignore the need to engage the safety system of the brain before trying to promote new ways of thinking. The last things that should be cut from school schedules are chorus, physical education, recess, and anything else involving movement, play, and joyful engagement."

— Bessel A. van der Kolk, *The Body Keeps the Score: Brain, Mind, and Body in the Healing of Trauma*

The Body-Brain Connection

Evidence-Based Ways to Reduce Anxiety, Boost Engagement, and Increase Comprehension Across Classrooms

Gravity Goldberg

CORWIN

FOR INFORMATION:

Corwin
A SAGE Company
2455 Teller Road
Thousand Oaks, California 91320
(800) 233-9936
www.corwin.com

SAGE Publications Ltd.
1 Oliver's Yard
55 City Road
London EC1Y 1SP
United Kingdom

SAGE Publications India Pvt. Ltd.
Unit No 323-333, Third Floor, F-Block
International Trade Tower Nehru Place
New Delhi 110 019
India

SAGE Publications Asia-Pacific Pte. Ltd.
18 Cross Street #10-10/11/12
China Square Central
Singapore 048423

Vice President and
Editorial Director: Monica Eckman
Senior Director and Publisher,
Content & Product: Lisa Luedeke
Content Development Editor: Sarah Ross
Product Associate: Zachary Vann
Project Editor: Amy Schroller
Copy Editor: Colleen Brennan
Typesetter: C&M Digitals (P) Ltd.
Proofreader: Dennis Webb
Cover Designer: Gail Buschman
Marketing Manager: Megan Naidl

Printed and bound by CPI Group (UK) Ltd, Croydon, CR0 4YY

ISBN 9781071976913

This book is printed on acid-free paper.

25 26 27 28 29 10 9 8 7 6 5 4 3 2 1

Contents

SECTION II: How to Create More Body and Brain Connection

Appendices

Visit this book's companion website for downloadable resources.
https://companion.corwin.com/courses/bodybrainconnection

Acknowledgments

Thank you to my body. I have pushed you hard, ignored your wishes, and made you hurt, yet you keep going. You have allowed me to run at dawn witnessing vibrant sunrises, compete with teammates experiencing the power of we, and swim in numerous bodies of water feeling connection, flow, and life itself. I've lived so much of my days "in my head" that I often forget you are here and that you are me. Despite this lack of appreciation, you still keep me alive and allow me to open to possibilities.

Thank you to my family. My husband John has given me the gift of witnessing my life and of offering perspective. He has been there in the many moments when I lost connection to myself and also helped me regain it. He has also cooked too many meals to count, listened to my dreams, and offered a supportive "yes, and" to my vision. My son Leo has taught me how to be in awe. Because of him I've stared in amazement at the starry night sky, danced to terrible pop music in my pj's in the kitchen, and laughed at poop jokes until I needed to gasp for air. Becoming Leo's mom helped me reorient my relationship to my body and my brain.

Thank you to my colleagues at Gravity Goldberg, LLC. Julie McAuley, Dana Clark, Heather Frank, and Brianne Annitti are the best teachers and people I know. Our community shows me that authenticity and realness can happen amidst the backdrop of challenge.

Thank you to my thinking partner friends. Renee Houser, Lindsay Dibona, Lily Howard Scott, Rachael Gabriel, Elaine Shobert, and Michelle Bulla. You each offer friendship, smarts, and feedback. You kindly cheered and nudged in the places where I needed it.

Thank you to my parents. You saw my gifts, rooted for me, and instilled a hard work ethic and self-confidence that I am strong and powerful.

Thank you to my teachers Pat Miller and Carol James along with my classmates in Bodywork. I learned how to heal through my body alongside each of you. Thank you to my yoga teachers Betsy Ceva, Charlene Bradin, and Julie Lifton, who helped me learn to breathe.

Thank you to my students over the past twenty-five years, especially those who called upon me to view them in new ways. All of those bouncy, distracted, challenging moments helped me "get it" and get you.

Thank you to the team at Corwin. Lisa Luedeke is a visionary publisher, editor, and friend who believes in my work and helps me make it better. Sarah Ross and Zack Vann answered every question and helped make sure everything behind the scenes worked out. Thank you to Amy Schroller for her work as project editor, Colleen Brennan for thorough and thoughtful copyediting, and Megan Naidl for her marketing wisdom.

Thank you to Daryl Getman, photographer extraordinaire, who has magical eyes that can capture the small moments of learning in action. Thank you to Olivia Burke, who was able to translate my words into gorgeous illustrations.

Thank you to the Ramsey school district, who opened up their classroom for the photographs in this book allowing me to showcase their exceptional leaders, teachers, and students. I am grateful for the help of Carmen Lacherza, Melissa Aujero, Carisa Bartley, Jennifer Crawford, Daryl Derleth, Jennifer Glebocki, and Jennifer Mejia along with all of their students. Thank you to McGee Middle School in Berlin, CT for hosting the video shoot. I am grateful for Christopher Sullivan, Jennifer Cardines and her students, and Laurie Gjerpen.

PUBLISHER'S ACKNOWLEDGMENTS

Corwin gratefully acknowledges the contributions of the following reviewers:

Lydia Bowden
Language Arts Teacher / Assistant Principal, County Public Schools
Atlanta, GA

Hilda Martinez
RTI Coordinator; Early Literacy Resource Teacher
Chula Vista, CA

Elaine Shobert
Literary Coach
Monroe, NC

About the Author

Gravity Goldberg is an international educational consultant and author of ten books on teaching. *Mindsets and Moves* (Corwin Literacy, 2015) put her on the world stage with its practical ways to cultivate student agency, leading to speaking engagements and foreign translations of her work. She has twenty-five years of teaching experience, including positions as a science teacher, reading specialist, third-grade teacher, special educator, literacy coach, staff developer, assistant professor, educational consultant, and yoga teacher. Gravity holds a B.A. and M.Ed. from Boston College and a doctorate in education from Teachers College, Columbia University. Gravity is a certified yoga teacher and graduate of the Wilderness Fusion Body Work program. As the founding director of Gravity Goldberg, LLC, she leads a team that offers side-by-side coaching and workshops that focus on teachers as decision makers and student-led instruction.

Section

I

Why Focus on the Body and Brain Connection?

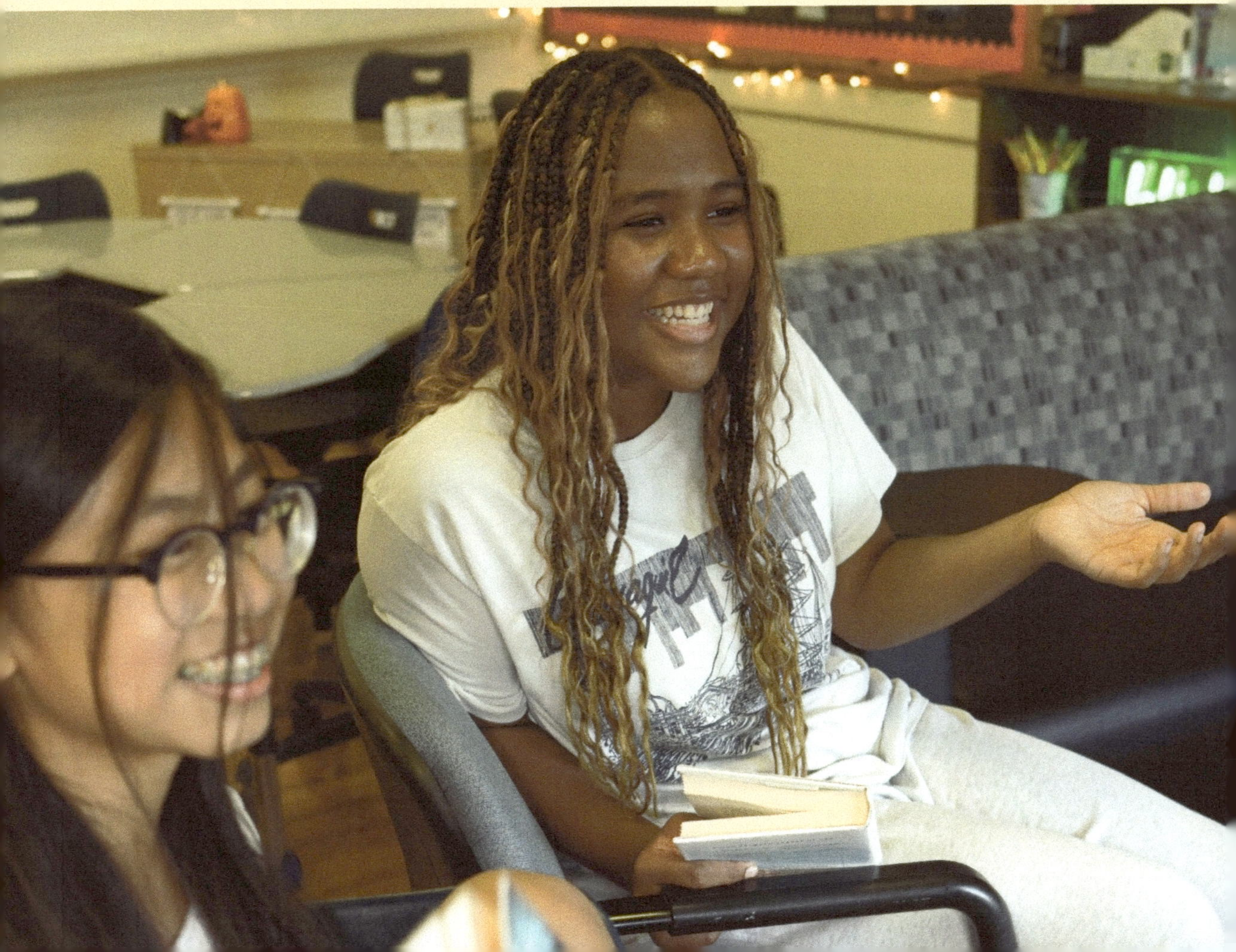

Chapter

1 Introduction

"A mindful approach to any activity has three characteristics: the continuous creation of new categories; openness to new information; and an implicit awareness of more than one perspective."

— Ellen J. Langer

As an educator, I have had countless experiences with students who seemed to need to move their bodies and through the movement were able to focus more, interpret more, and participate more in class experiences. See if any of these examples of students resonate with you.

Vin, a third grader, literally bounced up and down while sitting on his knees as he read and when he listened to a class read-aloud. At first I thought he was a fidgety kid who needed to learn to sit still, but after observing him for a few days the pattern was clear. Bouncing was Vin's way of self-regulating, staying focused, and also processing the joy he felt while reading. He loved books! The bouncing didn't match the still picture in my head of what I was taught a class should look like, but it didn't really distract anyone else and appeared to consistently help Vin. I decided to just let the bouncing continue and not bring attention to it. Vin's reading growth was huge that year. He maintained high levels of enthusiasm for books and never did stop bouncing.

Alex and Derek were both considered the most disruptive and most talkative students in the sixth-grade classroom. When put in groups with others they always took the group over and ended up arguing with their peers. Feelings were hurt, and the work didn't get done. Our plan to keep them separate meant that two groups were often in conflict at any point in the class period. My teaching partner and I decided to put these two students together in one group and see what happened.

First, we noticed they gravitated toward the window and second, they never sat down. They literally stood, paced, or rolled around on the floor and took many pauses to look out the window or move their bodies. They would spin, leap, or frog jump as they talked nonstop about their ideas. We listened and watched for the first few days and noticed there was no drama, no arguing, and the most sophisticated interpretations of the novel came from their partnership. We began to wonder why they couldn't just sit still and focus. It wasn't until we really listened to what they were saying that we realized they were very focused and very supportive of one another. Alex tended to leap when she heard an idea from Derek that she agreed with. When Derek looked out the window, it was often when the two felt stuck and needed to think more creatively. There were clear benefits to what looked like frenetic energy—supportive presence, creative thinking, focused attention, and willingness to take an intellectual risk. By pairing them up together, the two readers could move their bodies all they wanted without bothering their peers and also work together, at a fast and very moving pace, not being slowed down by or distracted by one another.

Tyler, a tenth grader who took English first period, often sat slumped over with his head down at the start of class. I'm sure he was tired; we all were at 7:42 a.m. When prompted to get up, walk to a cluster of desks in a circle, and pick up his book club materials, he did. As he faced his peers, he usually began to wake up and catch their energy. After a few minutes of discussion about the latest chapters the clubs had read, I looked over and noticed Tyler moving his hands, gesturing a lot, as the other students stared intently, leaning in. Then I saw nods, and another student picked up a copy of the text, located a part, and read it to the group seemingly adding textual examples to what Tyler had been saying.

When I walked over to listen, I noticed it was not just Tyler, as everyone in his group was using their bodies to participate in this conversation and develop some shared ideas. I saw hands flipping through pages, heads nodding, fingers pointing, hands jotting down notes, and feet tapping. I stayed a little longer to listen and observe and noticed that Tyler's gestures seemed to match the tone and content of what he was trying to explain. He discussed the relationship between two characters and used each hand to represent them. The idea that the characters' conflict was creating a lot of tension was represented in the way he moved his hands further away from each other. I don't think Tyler had any conscious awareness his hands were communicating his thinking, but nonetheless it was clearly happening.

Throughout my years as an educator, I have come to understand that learning happens in our **whole bodies**, not just in our heads. **Movement, both big and small, unconscious and conscious fuels our learning success.**

The ways I was taught to learn in school and at home acted as though my head was THE place where learning happens and the rest of my body's job was to stay out of the way. Sit up, in hard chairs, at desks, under harsh light, while remaining quiet and still. This was the case even though I spent my entire life playing sports. There was a clear divide between school, where my body was to be ignored, and sports, where my body was the focus. Nowhere was there a focus on considering the ways my body and mind worked together.

Years ago, when training for a marathon, I had the realization that when I went for runs on my own, often on wooded trails, I always generated creative ideas; I was brimming with them. I could map out an entire book, plan a trip, solve that problem from earlier in the week, and all while experiencing the joy and flow of ideas. I would come back from a run and immediately grab my notebook, trying to capture a fraction of the creativity that came with each stride. Other times I noticed that when I felt stuck with a problem and couldn't think of a next step, simply getting up from the table to walk to get water brought up several ideas that I had no access to while sitting.

This book has been a personal passion project of mine for so long. It started as a way to uncover more about myself while pursuing a yoga teacher certification after finishing up my doctoral work. Why did I love to move so much? Was there a connection between my own body-based experiences and my literacy life? What research could help me understand why movement was so tied to my creativity?

As I read research, I began to bring more curiosity and awareness beyond my own life and extend it to the students in the many classrooms I support. The abundance of research from a range of disciplines from linguistics to disability studies to psychology to neuroscience and embodiment all contributed pieces to my larger understanding that teaching and learning must not just focus on the mind but also on the body.

I've kept up with the ever changing landscape of evidence-based instruction, and while I am confident we know a whole lot about how children learn, there are far too many students who still struggle to read and write across the disciplines. This book is for those of us educators who know that learning is more nuanced than it is simple and that when we consider the whole student, including their bodies, we can be more effective teachers.

It turns out my body, which likes to move and even needs to move to feel safe, has a very large impact on all of the learning I have done across my life. I've discovered that our nervous system and our sensorimotor systems impact almost all of what we do as readers, writers, and thinkers. Our bodies don't have to be so often ignored in our instructional choices. I've also discovered that we don't necessarily need a new curriculum or instructional materials to make the most of brain and body integrated approaches. The ideas in this book can likely work with your current curriculum and are accessible to any teacher that is willing to look at the whole child.

WHO THIS BOOK IS FOR

Students read all day long, across subjects and contexts. For this reason, this book is geared toward all teachers who want to help students reduce anxiety about reading, learn to build stamina and focus, and develop comprehension in their given content area. Elementary teachers may witness students dealing with anxiety in very different ways than do secondary teachers, but the nervous systems in five-year-old bodies and fifteen-year-old bodies work the same. Likewise, distraction may look different in a Grade 1 classroom, where students roll around the floor or play with books instead of reading them, than it does in an eighth-grade classroom, where students pretend to read, holding the book in front of their faces without turning the page. Knowing what may cause the lack of stamina and what we can do to support students is something that all teachers can benefit from learning. This book is for any educator who has unanswered questions about what to do to support students with self-regulation and active learning and are curious how more awareness of the body's connection to learning can open up new possibilities.

HOW TO USE THIS BOOK

This book is program and curriculum neutral. This means that no matter what materials your district uses, you can apply the ideas and practices to your lessons. I offer you descriptions of research, instructional practices, and ideas for how you might apply these to your classroom. I do not offer you unit or lesson plans that align to a specific curriculum, but I do offer examples throughout the book of what this might look like when you model or when students are reading in class. You can read this book thinking about when the practices will be used in your classroom based on your particular curriculum. End-of-chapter charts summarize the practices and help you think about how you will use them.

Because this book is written for teachers across kindergarten through high school, some of the examples are elementary, some are middle school, and some are high school. I've varied the examples and photographs throughout the book so that no matter the age you teach you'll find some places that match your context. There will be places where you will have to reflect upon what this would look like with your specific students. Again, the end-of-section reflections are opportunities to think, share, and plan with your colleagues to create lessons for your specific students.

Resist the urge to file the ideas in this book as simply social-emotional learning. Yes, there are studies and practices that lean into psychology and sociology, but, as you will read in Chapter 2, comprehending is not just a cognitive skill. In order for students to pay attention to your lessons, focus on the text in their hands, and actually understand what they are reading, students need the ideas in this book.

The following table shows the book's key features and how you can use them.

<table>
<tr>
<td>
PRIME YOURSELF
Before you begin reading, notice some of your own body-based preferences as a reader.
• Do you like it quiet or do you prefer some background noise?
• What kind of furniture do you prefer to sit in as you read?
• Are you aware of the lighting? Do you like overhead

Prime Yourself

Where You'll Find Them: The beginning of every section

What They Are For: Gives you a quick personal experience with the section material and brings your attention to some key ideas the section will address

How to Use Them: Take a few minutes to do the priming experience and then pause. Reflect upon your own experience before reading on. Possibly jot a few notes for yourself.
</td>
<td>
WHY DOES SAFETY MATTER?

Questions

Where You'll Find Them: At the start of a new section

What They Are For: Helps you set the purpose for what kind of information you'll be reading about

How to Use Them: They can guide your thinking and notes by offering you landmarks that help you recognize a new chunk of information is coming.
</td>
</tr>
<tr>
<td>
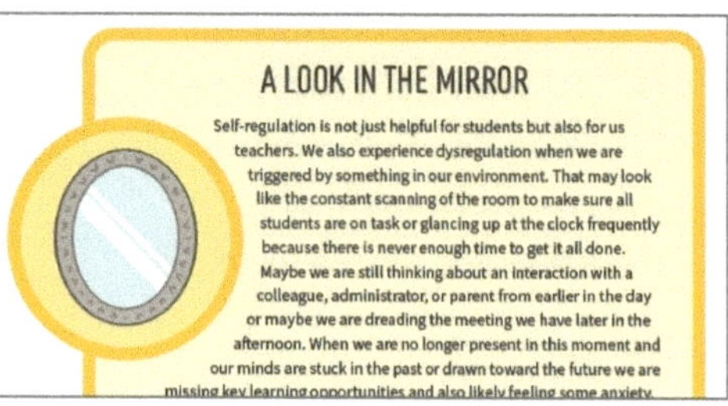
A LOOK IN THE MIRROR
Self-regulation is not just helpful for students but also for us teachers. We also experience dysregulation when we are triggered by something in our environment. That may look like the constant scanning of the room to make sure all students are on task or glancing up at the clock frequently because there is never enough time to get it all done. Maybe we are still thinking about an interaction with a colleague, administrator, or parent from earlier in the day or maybe we are dreading the meeting we have later in the afternoon. When we are no longer present in this moment and our minds are stuck in the past or drawn toward the future we are missing key learning opportunities and also likely feeling some anxiety.

A Look in the Mirror

Where You'll Find Them: Within chapters

What They Are For: Self-reflection spaces, prompts, and ideas for you to think about how the research applies to your own life and teaching

How to Use Them: Pause, reflect, and try out some of the ideas on your own or with your colleagues.
</td>
<td>

Illustrations

Where You'll Find Them: Throughout chapters where more abstract or scientific ideas are presented

What: Helps you create a mental model of a complex, nuanced, or hard-to-picture idea

How to Use Them: Synthesize the written information with the illustration to get a more complete understanding of the concept.
</td>
</tr>
</table>

Photographs

Where You'll Find Them: Throughout the chapters where concrete teaching ideas are described

What They Are For: Helps you picture what the idea looks like with teachers and students in real classrooms

How to Use Them: Synthesize the written description with the photograph to help you plan for what this might look like in your classroom.

Types of Threats Readers May Experience

Type	Example
confidence	I can't do this.
expectations	I will let my teacher down.
identity	People might find out I am not a good reader.
judgment	My teacher doesn't think I am a good reader.
punishment	I am going to get in trouble if I can't do this.
skill	I don't know how to ask for help.
social belonging	My peers won't include me if I can't do this.

Evidence-Based Practices

Where You'll Find Them: Following the research descriptions

What They Are For: Makes the research applicable and actionable

How to Use Them: Keep a running list of practices you want to try out. Notice what is confirming and what is new for you.

A SUMMARY OF KEY IDEAS FROM CHAPTER 3

In this section we examined what anxiety may look and feel like and how it impacts readers. We learned about the autonomic nervous system and its role in regulation. By including grounding practices, we can proactively support all students, especially the ones who experience stress and would benefit from more co-regulation.

A Summary of Key Ideas

Where You'll Find Them: At the end of chapter

What They Are For: Summarizes the research in a bullet list to help you remember key concepts

How to Use Them: Compare the list to your own notes, notice the elements that most resonate with you that you want to remember and discuss.

A SUMMARY OF PRACTICES FROM CHAPTER 3

Practice	Reflection Questions	When and Where I May Use This
Track your own nervous system by checking in with yourself using the Autonomic Ladder (see page ___).	How am I feeling right now? What might my body need to feel safe and secure?	
Acknowledge the ways students may be experiencing reading as threatening. Make a	Which of these experiences can you relate to? How do you know when you are	

A Summary of Practices

Where You'll Find Them: At the end of the chapter, after the research summary

What They Are For: Lists the practices from the chapter in an easy-to-reference chart

How to Use Them: Read the list, note which practices are already in place in your classroom and mark which ones you will want to try with your students.

Section II looks at how to incorporate more body and brain integrated practices into your teaching and why they work. Section III helps you put the information together to consider what a period looks like and how you can develop some new teaching habits to implement the practices you read about.

FIVE KEY IDEAS

In this book, there are five key ideas that ground us in a body and brain integrated approach. There is a chapter that focuses on each of the following key ideas, takes you through the research base, and offers some evidence-based practices to try.

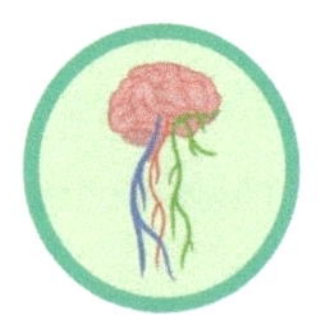	1. Students learn when they feel safe.
	2. Students' bodies help them handle difficulty.
	3. Students learn through movement.
	4. Students use gesture to create and communicate understanding.
	5. Students learn in places.

WHERE THE IDEAS IN THIS BOOK COME FROM

The research I cite comes from labs as well as more authentic environments. This was important to me as a researcher and as an educator because I value both the lab setting with its scientific measurement tools as well as the authentic landscape of classrooms and spaces where the teaching and learning happen. The research participants in the studies I cite range in age from babies through adults, and some of the settings are K–12 classrooms, college classrooms, medical facilities, and camps, to name a few. This range of participants and settings meant I had to interpret the results for what it could look like in K–12 classrooms.

I took the research findings and tried them out with students and teachers across different schools and populations. There is no possible way I could generalize all of the research findings to your exact students. I trust that you will take the ideas in this book and test them out with your own students, participate in practitioner research, and share your findings with your larger education community.

What I found from this deep dive into the body's role in learning is that we know so much. We know that our nervous system and sensorimotor systems play a vital role in all learning practices. Yet, we also have so much more to learn. We don't tend to even acknowledge the body's role in learning. We don't have common language to talk about bodies in school settings beyond "behavior" and outdated notions of dualism that leave our bodies silent and passive. This book will help us bring more awareness and develop more language to talk about bodies in classroom spaces beyond issues of behavior and control.

MY HOPES

What I hope most is that this book gets you excited to notice the role the body plays in learning. I also hope we recognize that our bodies are deeply connected to all the teaching and learning we do and that when we pay more attention to our bodies and our students' bodies, we can all feel safer, more integrated, and more successful as readers, writers, and thinkers.

As humans, many of the ideas in this book will feel intuitive and "right" based on your own sensorimotor and nervous system experiences. As educators who have been socialized to ignore our bodies, we may also resist some of the ideas and label them as radical. You are not wrong; it is radical to recognize that our brains are not computers, that the ways we move do impact our experiences, and that what we tend to believe may not actually be true. I am excited for you to experience this book as a learner, as a teacher, and as a whole person who has a mind AND a body.

Chapter 2

Students Learn Through Their Bodies

"Our unapologetic embrace of our bodies gives others permission to unapologetically embrace theirs."

— Sonya Renee Taylor

PRIME YOURSELF

Before you begin reading, notice some of your own body-based preferences.

- Do you like it quiet, or do you prefer some background noise?
- What kind of furniture do you prefer to sit in as you read?
- Are you aware of the lighting? Do you like overhead or a side lamp?
- What kind of posture do you take on as you read? Do you curl up, stretch out, sit up straight, or slump?
- What is around you in your environment? Windows? Screens? Other people?
- Do you enjoy drinking or eating while you read?

This body-based check-in with yourself helps you become more aware of what your body prefers. The answers might also surprise you if you are not used to asking these sorts of questions. For example, you may tend to sit in a room with the television on, but do you prefer that or is it just a habit? Or you may notice you find yourself slumped over the table as you read, almost hunched at the waist. Does your body enjoy this posture, or is this just a sign of fatigue setting in? By honestly reflecting on how your body feels and what it likes as a reader, it sets you up to be even more intentional to make choices the next time you sit (or stand) to read.

You can pose similar sorts of questions to your students to help create the right environment for reading, writing, and thinking in the classroom. This can also help students set up learning areas in their homes to help them establish routines that consider their bodies and invite them to want to open that book.

Ever since the one-room schoolhouse, many teachers have been encouraged to get control of the class by making sure students are sitting still, often in rows, with their heads down working. This is a myth really, that our bodies need to be removed from the learning process. This goal of having a quiet and still classroom of students might not just be unrealistic, but it may also be getting in the way of learning. Much of school seems to be about making student bodies as minimally included as possible, almost as if the bodies could be absent and the learning would go on. We saw firsthand during Covid-19 remote learning how this form of disembodied learning went. Educators found out how important students' bodies are in the learning process when they disappeared behind video cameras that were shut off or disabled.

There are a few reasons why these beliefs about bodies not being needed in learning came to be. The following list is a highly simplified summary of really big concepts that can help us understand how much of what is seen as common sense and taken for granted knowledge, such as the need for students to sit quietly and focus as they read, is based on theories developed in rationalism (Fodor et al., 1974). Let's look at how our understanding of learning and literacy has shifted across time.

> *Dualism:* In the 1600s French philosopher Descartes described the Cartesian model of mind and body dualism. This led to the belief that mind and body are separate entities. He believed that the mind is the location of our intelligence. Lessons in school, therefore, should focus on the child's mind.
>
> *Rationalism:* The next century brought in rationalism, the belief that knowledge could be gained through reasoning. Later the cognitive sciences were led by pioneers who believed that the body did not participate in cognitive processes (Chomsky, 1965, 1975). This is also where the metaphor of our minds working like computers stems from. School therefore, became the place where we focus on the mind and keep the body quiet.
>
> *Neuroscience:* Advances in research methods helped with the discovery of how connected the brain and body really are. We now know that the mind is integrated into the body's sensorimotor systems (Barsalou, 1999, 2008). Neuroscience studies have demonstrated that understanding objects, spatial awareness, experiences, and settings, as well as thinking about these concepts, activates sensorimotor responses in the body (Pulvermüller, 1999, 2003). Our bodies impact our thinking, and our brains are not really like computers at all.

> *Embodiment:* This view of learning acknowledges the interconnectedness of mind and body. It aims to reunite the body and mind and look at learning through an integrated approach that doesn't leave any parts behind. A core belief of embodiment studies is that learning is grounded in sensory and motor experiences (Engel et al., 2013; Mahon & Hickok, 2016). Our bodies not only participate in learning but may drive it.

Often researchers discuss this shift from dualism to embodiment as a shift from top-down to bottom-up learning. In the top-down model the mind is the place where all thinking and learning first happens and then that thinking leads to physical movement. In the bottom-up model the body has physical experiences and sensory input that travels through the body and influences the mind's thinking. At this point, there is agreement between most fields that the whole body plays a role in learning, but depending on the field of study, some researchers hold onto a top-down model where the mind is "king" while other fields of study have shifted to a bottom-up model that acknowledges the key role our bodies play in learning from the start.

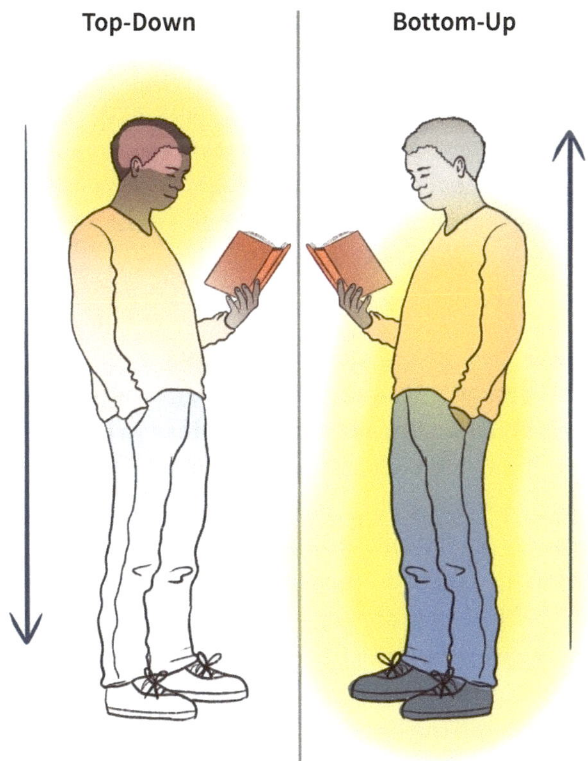

Many of us teachers have been taught to control the bodies of students. This may look like students lining up while moving through the hallways, silently walking out of the building for fire drills, and raising their hands before speaking. These practices may be totally necessary in order to make the school function, to help students get to lunch on time, and to create physical safety. There is a practicality that this form of control warrants. Sometimes, though, we have gone too far in controlling and limiting the bodies of students. If school or classroom policies don't allow students to use the restroom, get any time outdoors, or simply stand up and move during an entire period, we are denying the very humanity of students and possibly limiting their potential. I say this not with condemnation and judgment but more as a call for reflection. As you read this book you will understand the real need for students' bodies to be included in instructional planning and decisions.

While an in-depth look at the role bodies have played historically in education settings is beyond the scope of this book, I must acknowledge that students' bodies have been both largely ignored in their role in learning and also the cause of oppression for groups of students. Depending on the race, gender, sexuality, and perceived disability of the bodies of students, many inequities have been created. I suggest you read more about issues with harm and healing being done to students based on the perceptions of their bodies by studying the work of Taylor (2018) in *The Body Is Not an Apology*, Coppola (2023) in *Literacy for All*, Shalaby (2017) in *Troublemakers*, Love (2023) in *Punished for Dreaming*, and Annamma (2017) in *Pedagogy of Pathologization*. I am suggesting that we welcome students' bodies into the classroom as an important part of our classroom community that will help them. Also we must be aware that all of our students' bodies must be safe, not just the ones that match mainstream ideas of "normal."

In this book you'll come to see the abundance of evidence from neuroscience, environmental science, psychology, sociology, linguistics, and education that our bodies are not extra baggage we carry around, needing to be ignored. **It is the interconnectedness of our bodies and minds that lead to learning success.** We have so much to gain from this model of learning about the role our bodies play in learning. It is not helpful for the myth of absent bodies to continue because it both ignores the real experiences students are having in their bodies and robs teachers of vital body-based tools they could be using to be even more effective. We can use all of the available resources, including ones related to our bodies, to help students learn to read, write, and think well. If we continue as a field to ignore the body-based aspects of learning, we are missing a huge opportunity for self-regulation, more focused attention, an ability to tackle challenges, and deepen comprehension of ideas. As you continue reading this book, think about Descartes' famous line "I think, therefore I am" being replaced by the motto at the Laboratory for Embodied Cognition at Arizona State University that states, "I act, therefore I think."

LEARNING SHIFTS AND THE BODY

Listen to lunchroom conversations, read newspaper articles, and click on social media feeds and you'll likely get inundated with soundbites about why students today are struggling. While theories abound about what programs need to be purchased, what models need to be banned, and who really knows what is best, the arguing leads to stalemates at best and massive confusion at least.

Much of the narrative of what is "wrong" is really just signaling a shift. Students today are living in a different context than when we were kids. Think about your own life changes. Many of us used to buy tapes or CDs, we had to wait all week to watch our favorite show or figure out how to record it, and we had to call our friends on the phone to connect. In the past few decades technology has created massive shifts in how we learn, what we read, how we connect, and oftentimes how we feel. These shifts happened much more rapidly than our shifts in curriculum and instructional practice. While many authors, social media influencers, and policymakers theorize and often lament these shifts, we really only have two choices: (1) wait for students to shift back or (2) make some shifts ourselves. Believe me, I know it would be a whole lot easier for us educators if students showed up differently tomorrow, but in all likelihood that is not going to happen. So, let's look at these shifts as opportunities to consider new angles, new practices, and start including the body and brain in our decisions.

We know a lot more today than ever before about what happens in the brains of students as they read. We have data about the effectiveness of some models of instruction, and literacy seems to be getting the much needed attention it deserves because it impacts many aspects of students' lives. Yet, young children still struggle with literacy across the content areas, students tend to read less the longer they are in school, and many adults in this country do not read books and struggle with digital literacy skills. Unfortunately, the challenges with teaching students to read and then creating the contexts where older students and adults want to read is not simple. Let's look at some of the shifts in schools today and begin to consider the body and brain connection to them.

- Students are more culturally and linguistically diverse.
- Technology has radically shifted what we read, how we read, and where we read.
- Our understanding of instructional practices has shifted due to interdisciplinary research findings.
- Students (and teachers) today are experiencing high levels of stress and anxiety.

Personalization

Reading does not exist in a vacuum. It is personal and contextual and always informed by who the reader is (their identities, purposes, and contexts), what text they are reading (type, author perspective, purpose), and what task they are working on (summarize a story for a friend, plan for steps of a science experiment, or identify the key details in a math word problem). This means literacy exists in particular places, in particular times, and in particular people's bodies. It is never exactly the same for everyone or the same across contexts. I don't mean that each person's brain is doing something different, as we know that certain regions of the brain take on specific jobs. I mean our prior knowledge, experiences, and beliefs impact the sense we make of the text. The sensory experience we have while reading also impacts every element of how we think as we read.

Reading across contexts involves more than cognition. How a student perceives struggle, their stamina for focused attention, and their beliefs about themselves also impact how they read. For example, a student might feel confident when reading a story in language arts but insecure when reading technical descriptions in a science article.

The following table helps us examine the many aspects of what it means to be a reader across content areas and contexts. This table helps us look at students in multidimensional ways and see them more holistically. If they are struggling, it may not just be about cognitive skills and can include any or many of the following areas.

Identity	Who I am and the communities I am a part of impact the meaning I make from the text.
Purpose	Why and what I am reading impact how I read (recipe, comic, lab report, beach read, etc.).
Agency	I know how to choose what I read and how I interact with a text.
Mindset	I see myself as a reader.
Transfer of Skills	I use my skills learned in one area in other reading experiences.
Connections	I bring all my experiences and knowledge to help me understand a text or topic.

Some students have learned to view their cultural practices and knowledge as irrelevant in school-based learning experiences. This view may be created when we don't explicitly name all of these parts of being a reader listed in the previous table. If students think reading is only a technical skill, they may miss opportunities to use their social and cultural knowledge to help them read people, experiences, and texts. "Pedagogies should be more than responsive of, or relevant to, the cultural experiences and practices of young people—it requires that they support young people in sustaining the cultural and linguistic competencies of their communities while simultaneously offering access to dominant cultural competence" (Paris, 2012, p. 95).

According to data from 2021, 5.3 million students (10.6 percent) in the U.S. K–12 school system are receiving English language support (National Center for Education Statistics, 2024). Many more students who are multilingual do not qualify for English learning support in school, because they are already proficient in English and another language. There is an abundance of research that shows multilingualism is an asset and helps with creativity, cognitive flexibility, and higher levels of abstract thinking, among many other benefits (Office of English Language Acquisition, n.d.). By providing opportunities for students to bring their multilingual knowledge and practices into the classroom it helps them become stronger readers, writers, and thinkers across content area experiences.

This book is filled with ideas for how you can encourage, model, and prompt students to use their bodies to understand oral and written language. It also explains how to integrate the body when producing language to share with others.

Multimodal Learning

For several decades, scholars have argued for a more expansive view of literacy as multimodal. “Multimodal literacy is a process of generating meaning in transaction with multimodal texts including written language, visual images, and design features from a variety of perspectives to meet the requirements of particular social constructs” (Serafini, 2014). This means we can read a film, a podcast, an image, a landscape, and a body, not just printed letters on the page, and we do this for personal and social reasons. In many science, social studies, math, and art classes students are spending time reading, but it may not be printed words in a book. This is still reading. Our purpose drives what we read and the ways we read. Our bodies are experiencing sensorimotor input as they view, listen, notice, and note across modes. All literacies include the integration of our bodies and our brains.

Research in multiliteracies shows we need to include audio, gestural, oral, spatial, tactile, and visual literacies as we assess students’ competencies (Cope, 2015). When students develop language comprehension, it is almost always aided by body language comprehension as they view facial expressions and gestures, as well as social comprehension, as they try to interpret how the other person feels. Reading in a multimodal way is helped by our body’s ability to make sense of what is said, unsaid, how it is said, and what it really means. This includes subtext and intention. Some of the unanswered questions teachers have about why students struggle to comprehend a text involve more attention and awareness on reading what another person’s body is saying, not just their words.

Embodied Learning

Despite many findings and helpful conclusions from research studies, many students still struggle to read well across every content area. Researcher Kelly B. Cartwright (2023) describes what data have shown about reading challenges. "Traditional predictors of reading comprehension (word reading and language comprehension skills described by the simple view; Gough & Tunmer, 1986) only explain about *half* of the difficulties experienced by students with reading comprehension difficulties" (p. 42). While it is helpful and hopeful that researchers have studied the impact of word reading and language comprehension skills on reading, this also reveals that the other half of difficulties may be missed or remain invisible. What about the other half of students who have had explicit instruction in word reading and language comprehension that still struggle with reading?

Duke and Cartwright (2021) updated the simple view of reading that most research is based upon to create an active view of reading. In their model they include active self-regulation as a necessary component to skilled reading. Teachers often have a host of questions about how to support the many students who need support with active self-regulation. These reading challenges do not exist solely in language arts classrooms. If students struggle as readers, they likely struggle across the content areas since reading is embedded in much of what happens across their day.

My contribution to this discussion aims to extend our understanding about how students' nervous system and sensorimotor systems also play a role in reading. This integrated and whole body view of reading builds upon the active view to add in embodied lenses. This means that active self-regulation can happen only when the body feels safe and is not in fight, flight, or freeze mode, and that students' sensorimotor system is involved in all aspects of learning. The way the body feels and moves (turning the page of a print book, gesturing as they explain their thinking) along with the ways language is processed in the sensorimotor system (simulation and enactment theories) are all important components of how we understand what it means to read. By including the whole body we have a more holistic view of students and a broader range of tools to choose from.

Dysregulation

Approximately two-thirds of American children will experience at least one traumatic event by the time they are sixteen, according to research cited by the Substance Abuse and Mental Health Services Administration (n.d.). At least sixty percent of students have been impacted by adverse childhood experiences (ACEs), which have been shown to create chronic stress (Campaign for Trauma-Informed Policy and Practice, 2022). This means that all of us teachers have students in the classroom that may experience dysregulation. Even students who don't have high ACE scores often show up in class dysregulated due to everyday stressors such as peer drama, pressure to succeed at all costs, and too much time spent indoors or eating sugary foods that overload their system.

If we are honest with ourselves, many of us teachers are also showing up to class in dysregulated bodies. This might be due to school-related issues such as parent pressure; shifts in expectations from the central office; lack of clarity and support from administrators, who often are overworked themselves; or unrealistic deadlines and workload. Since we also have lives outside of school, our personal dysregulation might also be due to family issues, financial issues, health issues, or any number of other stressors that we face daily. Even if we have the best of intentions to meditate, eat well, and leave our feelings at the classroom door, our bodies still hold onto it all. As van der Kolk (2014) says, "Our bodies keep the score." When we are dysregulated we can't simply think ourselves back to regulation.

So much of what appears to be defiance or incompetence is the result of a student experiencing a nervous system response that shuts down their higher level thinking and memory and activates the threat response. This might look like off-task behaviors, constant fidgeting, or that "deer in the headlights" look.

We experience this nervous system response when our body gets a flood of the stress response chemicals. We can learn to recognize triggers, self-regulate our nervous system responses, and co-regulate with others. Only when we are out of that fight, flight, or freeze state can we more fully access our thinking and memory centers and be primed for learning. Yes, our brains will be the place where a lot of this happens but only while it is connected to the rest of our body. Learning happens when our nervous system is *experiencing safety* and the calmness that comes with it.

You likely wear many hats, which may include educator, caregiver, partner, friend, neighbor, and so many more. Juggling these many responsibilities and also experiencing the desire to support a classroom of students can feel overwhelming. This overwhelm comes in waves of stress where it is literally hard to think straight. This is because when we experience stress our bodies flood with cortisol, which activates parts of our brain to go into hypervigilance. This is the fancy word for constantly scanning our environment for things we think need to be addressed. It means our attention is spread to everything and everyone around us, except we often lose sight of ourselves. While hypervigilance is an important tool to have when you need to be super aware of possible threats, it is not helpful when it becomes our baseline and typical way of being. Take a look at this chart and notice which of these stress-related experiences resonates with you. I divided the adult and student experiences so you can notice just how similar they are.

Adults' Experience of Feeling Stress	**Students' Experience of Feeling Stress**
• Having nervous energy/jitters • Making to-do lists that never end • Inability to fall asleep or stay asleep • Difficulty staying focused • Feeling annoyed at people around you • Daydreaming about rest or escape • Wanting people to leave you alone • Feeling alone • Using sugar and caffeine to keep going when you need to pause • Drinking alcohol or using drugs to numb • Scrolling on social media	• Having nervous energy/jitters • Inability to fall asleep or stay asleep • Difficulty staying focused • Feeling annoyed at people around you; irritability • Daydreaming and zoning out • Wanting people to leave you alone • Feeling alone • Avoidance • Asking lots of questions • Waiting for an adult to come help you get started • Shutting down as soon as things get hard • Spending every free moment on devices and social media

Students can also show up in our classrooms feeling stuck. When students get that stuck feeling, it is not usually solved by simply telling them with words what they can do. Feeling stuck is also a nervous system response and a sign of being in "freeze" mode. Take a look at this list and think about students in your class.

Students' Experience of Feeling Stuck

- Ruminating on the past
- Worrying about the future
- Second-guessing
- Staring off into space
- Asking for clarification right after your teaching
- Shrugging shoulders as responses
- Wanting adult approval for every step of their work
- Waiting for an adult to take them through every step

This combination of student and possibly teacher dysregulation impacts teaching and learning. As teachers, we don't have control over district-level systems, but we do have control over the lenses we use to view ourselves and our students. In Chapter 3 of this book, I explain what is going on when students are dysregulated, what it may look and feel like, and I offer ideas of how we can help. As an added bonus, there are tips for helping ourselves as educators too. We'll look at the autonomic nervous system and understand its key role in students' lives.

CLASSROOM SNAPSHOT OF A BODY AND BRAIN CONNECTED LESSON

Now that I have spent pages describing the shifts teachers face, I know you are itching to figure out what to do and how to do it. As a preview of the next few chapters I'll end by describing what an actively engaged classroom of students could look like that includes the brain and body connection. This is just one general example. Instead of reading this like an exact lesson planning framework, which it is not, look at the parts of the lesson. Make sure there is time to ground, gather, make a plan, share, and reflect, as these are important elements that help our teaching stick. You may call them something else or put them in a different order than I have described. This is not a formula, so feel free to adapt the parts and apply them to your current structures and programs. Section II will dive deeper into the many ideas listed in the snapshot that follows.

Part of the Lesson	Example
Ground	The teacher takes the first minute of class to lead students in a grounding experience. Once their bodies are calm and primed to learn, they can begin the lesson (see Chapter 3).
Gather	Students gather close in a semi-circle around the teacher, facing out the window (see Chapter 7). Some stand, some are sitting at tall tables, some sit in chairs, some sit on the floor, and all of them have the option of moving. A few may rock back and forth, and some may have a "fidget" in their hands. As long as they don't disturb others, students make choices about what their bodies need to focus.
Teach	The teacher uses words, visuals, and gestures in their teaching. Students are encouraged to use one of the movements already taught in class to quickly summarize what they learned from the teacher. This could be naming the parts as they point to an imaginary chart in the air, creating a gesture to go along with the lesson's topic, or listing what they learned as they touch each finger on their hand in a counting motion (see Chapter 5).

(Continued)

(Continued)

Part of the Lesson	Example
Make a Plan	Students are paired up with a peer that they trust. They take a minute or two to make a plan for the period. This reinforces and supports executive functioning skills and helps students feel ready to tackle the challenges of the day (see Chapter 4).
Read/Write/ Think/Do	Depending on the focus of the lesson, students find a spot that works for them and begin their work (see Chapter 7). As they read, write, think, and do they will be coached by their teacher, who has been implementing a variety of body and brain-based strategies (see Chapter 5).
Share	Either partway through the work time and/or at the end, students meet with their partners and share what they learned. They are prompted to use words, visuals, and their bodies in their explanations. Students are spread out and may act out, use gestures, and/or incorporate manipulatives as they share (see Chapter 5).
Reflect	As the period comes to an end, students are given time to reflect on how they are feeling, what they learned, and what next steps may be. This time reinforces the executive function skills of planning and self-monitoring. It also integrates the body and brain connection and helps them come full circle from the plan they made.

Step inside a body-brain connected lesson focused on reading for main ideas in nonfiction texts. Notice the parts of the lesson: Ground, Gather and Teach, Read and Talk, Share and Reflect.

A SUMMARY OF KEY IDEAS FROM CHAPTER 2

This chapter frames the purpose for the rest of this book and makes the argument that students will be more successful if their bodies and brains are considered when we plan instruction.

- The whole body, not just the brain, impacts reading and learning.
- Letting go of the idea that students learn best when they are still and quiet opens up much more possibility and aligns with research from neuroscience and embodiment.
- When we consider the ways social and cultural knowledge impacts learning, we expand what it means to be a learner and get a more holistic view of students.
- By incorporating more multimodal reading experiences across content areas that include video, audio, and images, along with print, we support students in what it means to be a reader in today's context.
- We can expand our view of reading to include our nervous system and sensorimotor systems.
- Stress has a large impact on our ability to teach and students' ability to learn. When students' stress dysregulates them, they cannot process what we teach them.
- We can plan instruction using a more body and brain connected approach that acknowledges the role that both play.

Section

II

How to Create More Body and Brain Connection

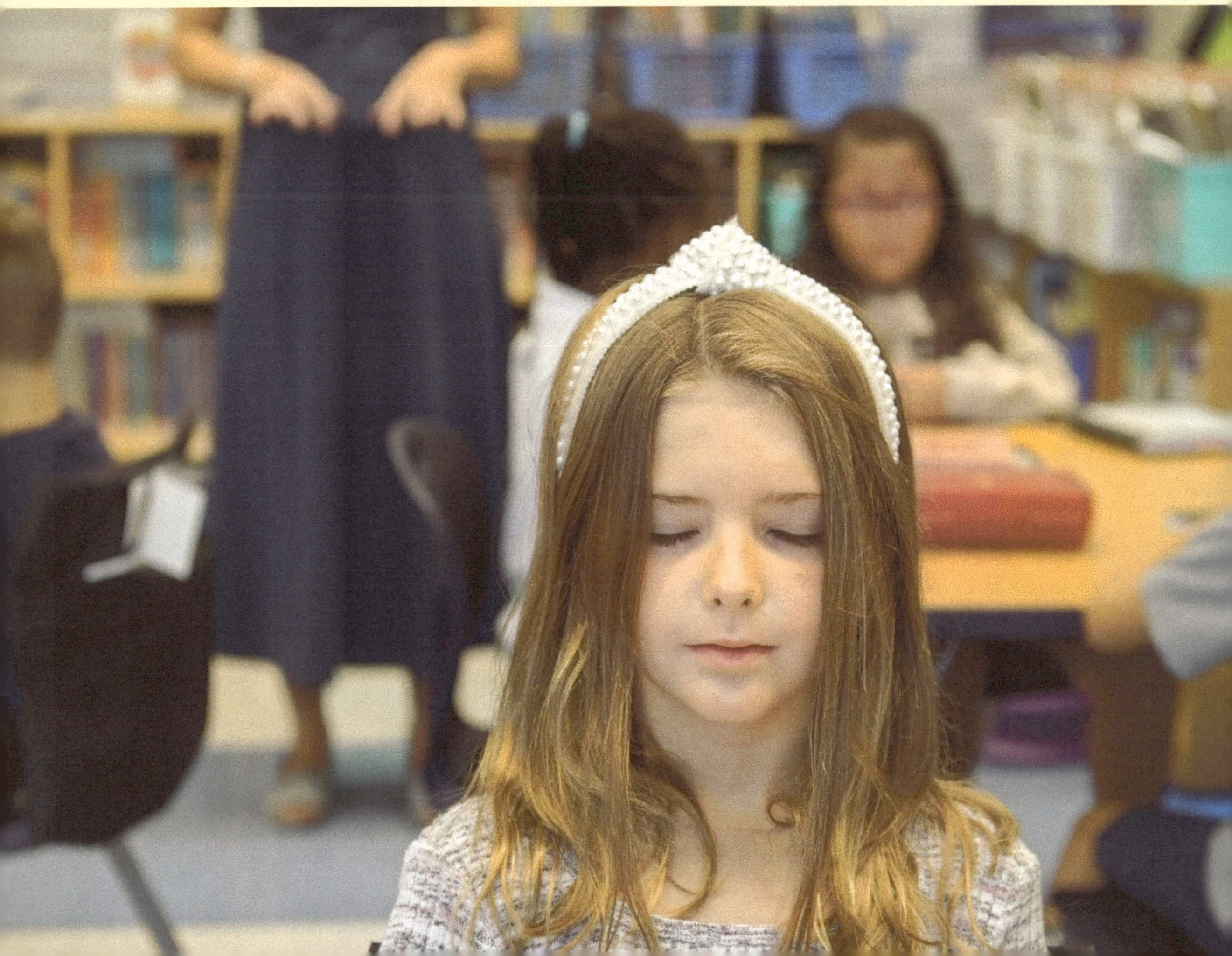

Chapter 3

Students Learn When They Feel Safe

"With our first breath, we embark on a lifelong quest to feel safe in our bodies, in our environments, and in our relationships with others."

— Dana (2023, p. 5)

PRIME YOURSELF

If you prefer to listen to this exercise as a guided practice you can find the audio here.

qrs.ly/zwgcxes

As you begin this section take three slow deep breaths. Try to exhale slowly, noticing your ribs moving up and down with each breath. Put both feet on the ground as you do this, feeling the contact between the soles of your feet and the floor. Look up for a minute and notice something in the room that feels familiar—maybe it is a lamp, a favorite pen, your notebook, a picture on the wall. If you are near a window, look outside and notice the movement of the trees, the shape of the clouds, the color of the sky. This awareness experience can take thirty seconds to one minute. Notice yourself physically settling into your body. Now begin to read.

Taking a minute to get yourself physically ready and calm and easing any potential anxiety is helpful for all of us, not just students. Even if you were not feeling anxious as you sat down to read, it still helps you check in and prime your body for learning. It builds a habit that you start with intention and makes it more likely you will support your students in this way too. We all experience anxiety and we can all benefit from intentional minutes throughout our day.

WHAT DO ANXIOUS STUDENTS LOOK LIKE?

Glancing over at the schedule of the day and seeing the word *reading* makes Timmy's stomach sink. His heart rate speeds up and his leg bounces up and down. Even though reading is not scheduled for another hour, he can't focus. His teacher is modeling a math strategy and then invites students to pair up to play a game but Timmy doesn't hear any of it. His nervous system puts him on high alert. Since he is only in the third grade and also has not learned ways to bring awareness or language to what is happening inside of him, he doesn't know how to ask for help. Instead he misses the teacher's cues and is left alone while everyone else pairs off and collects the materials they will need to play the game. It isn't until his teacher is tapping his arm gently that he even realizes where he is—in a classroom—and is able to hear what she has to say. He asks, "What?" and then shrugs his shoulders when told to get going.

Selma takes out her book and device, logs into Google Classroom, and waits for her teacher to begin the day's lesson. As her teacher reads aloud an excerpt from the short story the class has been analyzing the past few days, Selma's mind wanders. She daydreams about dance practice and the routine she is working on. She is looking in the direction of her teacher, holding a copy of the short story in her hands, but her attention is elsewhere. This tends to happen every time Selma is asked to read and especially when she is asked to analyze that reading. She seems to travel off to another place. Since she is not bothering anyone or distracting anyone, her teacher doesn't seem to notice. But she is terrified she'll be found out, because she is not really doing the reading, and that she'll get in trouble for being totally confused. Selma looks like a good student, but internally she is struggling with anxiety and puts all of her effort into looking competent instead of developing competence.

Students like Timmy and Selma are in all of our classrooms. Timmy presents as having attention issues and as highly distractible. Selma presents as a good student who never volunteers, contributes, or "lives up to her potential." Internally, both are having nervous system responses that get in the way of them focusing on reading, and both are experiencing dysregulation.

According to Griffin (1990) "anxiety may be defined as apprehension, tension, or uneasiness that stems from the anticipation of danger, which may be internal or external. . . . [I]t is important to remember that the manifestations of anxiety and fear in the body are the same." To some degree this definition of anxiety feels like a description of being a human of any age in a world full of potential threats. In fact, anxiety can sometimes be a useful tool when it doesn't overtake us or become our baseline experience. "Anxiety is a natural and often adaptive response to stress or potential threats. While some level of anxiety is normal and can even be helpful in certain situations, such as alerting us to potential dangers, excessive or persistent anxiety can become problematic and interfere with daily life" (Gleaves, 2023). Part of our job as teachers is recognizing when anxiety is an adaptive, occasional response and when it becomes a pattern that interferes with reading and learning.

As teachers we've been taught to focus on clarity, strategy, and purpose when designing lessons. We have learned the value of strong relationships with students. Yet, we often have not focused enough as a profession on anxiety and students' need for safety. When we bring this lens into classrooms, we notice nuances and can help students both avoid anxiety and learn to shift out of it as needed.

Anxiety in students may look like the following:

- Avoiding
- Daydreaming and staring off
- Fidgeting and leg bouncing
- Shrugging of shoulders
- Not knowing where or how to start
- Losing materials and being disorganized
- Asking for clarification
- Needing reassurance
- Head down on the desk
- Getting up and moving around

WHY DOES SAFETY MATTER?

Most if not all of the time, students are physically safe in classrooms. And yet, many students perceive threats in physiological ways on a regular basis. By safety I mean the ways a person's body is interpreting their environment and the degree to which they scan it for danger. In order to be calm and open enough to learn, to apply strategies, and to focus on learning, students must feel safe. Not just in their heads but also in their nervous systems.

When students' nervous systems perceive a potential threat, all of the attention that would be going to focused attention gets shifted to the physical setting and the people around them. This can lead us teachers to think the student is distracted and that a simple redirection of attention will do the trick. In reality, until their nervous system calms down, until they stop scanning the classroom for threats, they will not physically be able to focus, no matter how many times you redirect, call their name, or remind them of their task. No amount of verbal cues from you will help until the very real physiological reaction has run its course. As various health coaches remind us, "You can't think yourself out of a feeling."

Autonomic Nervous System

The autonomic nervous system is a two-branch system in our bodies that helps us survive. The two branches are the sympathetic and parasympathetic responses that travel down three possible pathways. The *sympathetic* branch starts in the brainstem and travels to the middle part of the spinal cord. This pathway prepares our body for action by triggering the release of adrenaline that can send us into fight or flight. The *parasympathetic* branch, which is connected to the vagus nerve, has two possible pathways. The vagus nerve begins in the brainstem at the base of the skull and travels in two directions—downward through the lungs, heart, diaphragm, and stomach and upward to connect with nerves in the neck, throat, eyes, and ears (Dana, 2023).

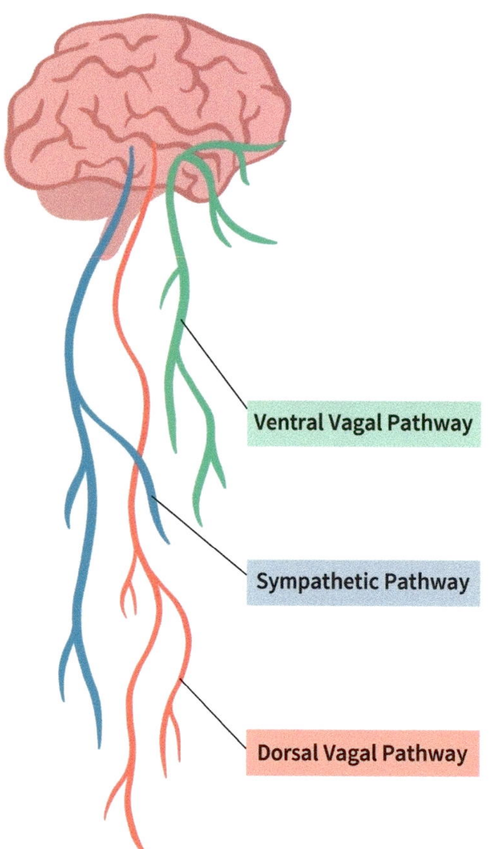

According to polyvagal theory (Porges et al., 1994) the vagus is divided into two parts, which correspond to two different physiological responses. One part, the ventral vagal pathway, responds to a sense of safety and supports our ability to feel secure and socially connected. The other part, the dorsal vagal pathway, responds to cues that are experienced as a threat. The dorsal vagal pathway takes us out of connection and puts us into a "protective state of collapse" (Dana, 2023, p. 6). This is often referred to as a freeze response where we feel shut down and numb.

Therapist and writer Dana (2023) uses a metaphor of a ladder to explain the autonomic nervous system. The top of the ladder is where we feel safe and able to socially engage with others. This experience often means, "I am connected to myself and can reach out to others" (p. 8). When we begin to sense a threat we move down the ladder and go

Autonomic Nervous System		
SYMPATHETIC	PARASYMPATHETIC	
	Dorsal Vagal	Ventral Vagal
Starts in brain stem ↓ Travels to middle of spinal cord	- lungs - heart - diaphragm - stomach	- neck - throat - eyes - ears
triggers release of ADRENALINE OR FIGHT! flight	FREEZE response - disconnection - shutdown	- sense of safety - security - social connection

into fight or flight. This sympathetic response often means I am "anxious or angry and feel the rush of adrenaline that makes it hard for me to be still. I listen for sounds of danger and don't hear the sounds of friendly voices" (p. 9). If we continue down the ladder to the dorsal pathway, we begin to shut down and feel trapped as "action taking does not work" (p. 9). It can be described as a feeling of being "hopeless, abandoned, foggy, too tired to think, act and the world is empty" (p. 9). The ladder metaphor helps us understand that this response is fluid and moves on a continuum. It can also be helpful to use it to teach students about how their autonomic nervous system works. (See Appendix A for a reproducible copy of the ladder image.)

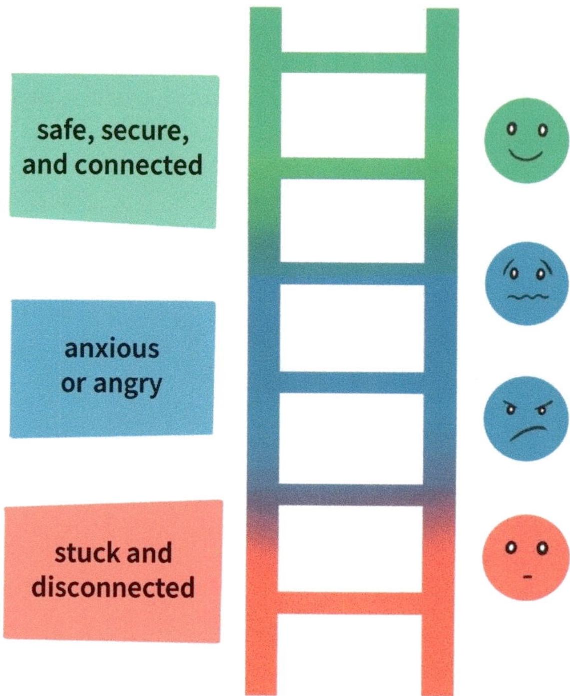

Use this image of the ladder to help students self-reflect on how they are feeling. They can name a color, point to the emoji, or use words to describe it.

Take a moment to reflect on your own nervous system experiences. We have all experienced situations where we were triggered into fight or flight (sympathetic response) and when we felt hopeless, lethargic, and stuck (parasympathetic dorsal response). What did you feel? Consider your heart rate, temperature, types of thoughts, speed of speech, and the decisions you made or were unable to make. Although each of us feels these two states in our own unique ways, we do tend to have similar physiological responses. In the following pages I will break down this process so we can better understand what is going on in our own bodies as well as in our students' nervous systems.

Neuroception

Dr. Porges (2009) developed polyvagal theory, which explains how safety is experienced in bodies. Our bodies are built to perceive our environments and form conclusions about them. We do this through a process called neuroception.

Neuroception is not just a visual and thinking based conscious process. It includes visceral feelings as well as environmental cues. Based on our process of neuroception, our bodies make conclusions that may trigger us into flight, flight, or freeze mode if a potential threat is discovered. Dr. Porges explains,

> Where does the intelligence come from that enables our nervous system to detect cues of safety, danger, or life threat? We can conceptualize this intelligence as a neural process involving higher brain structures that is not dependent on awareness or a conscious cognitive process. . . . [O]ur responses to risk are often immediate and virtually reflexive. To be functionally adaptive this process evolved outside the realm of conscious awareness. (Quoted in Devereaux, 2017, p. 28)

In other words, the process of neuroception is an unconscious process that happens beneath the level of awareness. Our bodies do this to keep us safe without the need to direct our attention to the process.

Think of a time you got a "gut feeling" that something was a threat. Maybe you were walking down the street and decided to avoid someone. Maybe you chose not to say something out loud that just didn't feel right. Maybe you paused to check in with yourself before hitting send on a text message. These are examples of ways your body gives you information. Neuroception has helped humans survive by providing a sensing mechanism to help keep us safe.

If you were walking in the woods and looked down and saw a large snake, you would likely have a visceral response. The next time you went on a hike you would be scanning the trail even more, looking for snakes. When you see a long and twisted branch on the ground, you may notice your heart race and your breath quicken. Neuroception would be helping you stay alert, be aware, and avoid possible danger.

When students are asked to pick up a text and begin reading, we teachers may not assess any threats, but that does not mean students are having the same neuroception experience. In fact, what seems totally safe to us might feel quite threatening to them. To complicate matters, what looks like task avoidance and attention issues might be a nervous system response students have little control over. The following table shows examples of types of threats students may experience. Most of these are never stated out loud but still inhabit students' bodies and minds. At the core of all of these fears is the fear of disconnection and of not belonging.

Types of Threats Students May Experience

Type	Example
Confidence	I can't do this.
Expectations	I will let my teacher down.
Identity	People might find out I am not good at this.
Judgment	My teacher doesn't think I am smart.
Punishment	I am going to get in trouble if I can't do this.
Skill	I don't know how to ask for help.
Social belonging	My peers won't include me if I can't do this.

You may want to use this table as a tool to normalize feelings and beliefs with students. For example, project this chart and explain how almost all of us have these beliefs from time to time. When we get stuck in one of these beliefs, we start to feel fear and then it triggers us to move down the autonomic ladder. Model how each example statement can be turned into positive self-talk, such as turning "I can't do this" into "I can do this." Our inner talk influences our feelings and our nervous system. Of course, we don't want to call on students or put them on the spot to share their beliefs in front of their peers. This practice is ideally focused on teacher modeling and offering time for self-reflection.

Another lesson idea is to use a story to identify character feelings and track them across the text. For younger students this could mean reading a picture book like *Let's Go Hugo!* by Angela Dominguez and prompting students to infer when Hugo is afraid, tell how they know, and point to where on the ladder he may be. For middle school students you may want to read *Ghost* by Jason Reynolds and track moments in the story when Ghost is moving along the autonomic ladder. You can chart what is happening, how he feels, how he shows his feelings, and then discuss any personal connections to his feelings. For high school students you could read *Clap When You Land,* by Elizabeth Acevedo and track the Rios sisters' movement along the ladder, along with comparing how they feel and how they are handling it. They could even give advice to each character based on what they learned about how to prime and calm the nervous system. For a sample lesson idea, see Appendix B.

HOW DOES THE NERVOUS SYSTEM IMPACT STUDENTS?

The next few pages will explain in more detail Porges's (2009) polyvagal theory and how it can help us understand students in our classrooms. For more information you can go to https://www.polyvagalinstitute.org/whatispolyvagaltheory.

Fight or Flight Response: Hyperarousal

We have all experienced "fight or flight" in our own bodies. When we use neuroception and detect a threat in our environments, we activate the sympathetic nervous system. This means we are mobilized for action and to try to get away from the threat. This nervous system response causes our bodies to increase our heart rate, blood pressure, hormones, and muscle tone (Porges, 2009). This is why we call it fight or flight—our bodies are literally gearing up to fight off an attack or run away from one.

When our sympathetic nervous systems are activated, we often become overwhelmed with emotions. In a school setting, students may be experiencing this fight or flight response and have some ability to recognize they cannot literally fight or flee. Instead this response may appear as agitation or aggression, meltdowns, and anxiety. Another response we cannot always see in students is hypervigilance. Hypervigilance is the constant scanning of the environment for potential threats (Porges, 2009). This might look like students paying attention to aspects of the classroom that are not relevant to the lesson, for example, facial expressions of peers, people walking by in the hallway, the temperature of the classroom, or your tone of voice but not its content. Sometimes students' hyperactivity and movement are also a part of the sympathetic nervous system response.

When students spend a lot of time in a sympathetic nervous system response, it can become their baseline way of being. This is described as a state of hyperarousal. When students are in a state of hyperarousal, they cannot possibly focus their attention on

HYPERAROUSAL

- sympathetic nervous system activated
- overwhelmed with emotions
- fight or flight response
- agitated or aggressive, meltdowns, anxiety, hyperactivity, and/or hypervigilance

your lesson, peer collaboration, or the text in their hands. The chart above can be found in Appendix C and can be used with students.

Freeze Response: Hypoarousal

If a student experiences a large amount of time in hyperarousal, they may shift into a state called "freeze response." This occurs when the parasympathetic nervous response is activated on the dorsal pathway and leads to low heart rate, low energy, and low muscle tone. The emotional response may look like depression and hopelessness. This is referred to as hypoarousal and is often identified by teachers when we see students shutting down and withdrawing from the learning experiences (Porges, 2009).

When students are in this state of hypoarousal, they have difficulty articulating their thoughts and often feel like they don't even have access to them. It can feel like "brain fog" and look like shoulder shrugs and responses of "I don't know" when asked a question. If a student spends a large amount of time in this state, they may feel disconnected from the class, from you, and from their peers.

When a student is trying to read in this freeze state, they often find themselves reading and not remembering anything they just read. Their mind may wander, causing them to reread often. This might also look like trouble synthesizing information and seeing how the pieces fit together as well as difficulty being able to annotate, discuss, or explain their thinking. As a teacher it can be quite frustrating to get little to no response from a student and it can feel challenging to connect with and build a relationship with students experiencing the freeze response. The following chart can be found in Appendix D and can be used with students.

HYPOAROUSAL

- freeze response
- withdrawn/shutdown
- disconnected from the world
- difficulty articulating thoughts

Window of Tolerance: Relaxed

When students are in a parasympathetic nervous system ventral vagal response, they feel relaxed and ready to learn. The physiological aspect of this state includes a normal heart rate and normal muscle tone. Emotionally students feel hopeful, curious, creative, and engaged (Dana, 2023). This happens when the student finds the classroom environment to be safe. This is often referred to as the "zone of tolerance." It does not mean there are no challenges to work through, but it does mean the student is able to socially engage from a place of calm and a sense of security.

When students are in this zone of tolerance, they have control over their emotions and thoughts, can be metacognitive about their reading process, and can make choices and take intentional action. This state of calm happens when the student's autonomic nervous system performs these two functions: "(1) assess risk, and (2) if the environment is perceived as safe, inhibit the more primitive limbic structures that control fight, flight, or freeze behaviors" (Porges, 2009, para. 21). The following chart can be found in Appendix E and can be used with students.

WINDOW OF TOLERANCE

- calm and secure
- environment perceived as safe
- social engagement system (ventral vagas) is activated
- control over emotions and thoughts
- optimal zone of arousal

"A more resilient individual will have a neuroception biased towards detecting cues of safety, while a less resilient individual will have a neuroception biased towards detecting threat" (Polyvagal Institute, n.d.). This means that students in the classroom may be in the exact same circumstance, read the exact same book, and have very different nervous systems responses. "If our neuroception is faulty, it sends a signal of danger when we're safe, or it sends a signal of safety when we're in danger. Faulty neuroception may be influenced by a history of adversity. For example, individuals with a history of severe adversity may find themselves habitually hypervigilant in anticipation of threats" (Polyvagal Institute, n.d.).

While the adversity students faced in the past may be related to reading difficulties, they don't need to be, in order to have a more sensitive response. Students bring all sorts of reading trauma and life trauma into the classroom, some of which we know about and much of which we don't. This impacts the student's identification of threat when asked to read, write about reading, or talk about reading.

Teacher's Beliefs

Now that we have an understanding of the autonomic nervous system and how students' actions are aligned to the state they are in, we can have empathy and also make some informed teacher choices. A few important beliefs can help us form strong relationships with students no matter their current nervous system response.

TEACHER BELIEFS AND MOVES THAT CAN LESSEN ANXIETY

- Bring a curiosity lens about what might be going on for each student.
- Make positive assumptions about students.
- Try not to make every day "game day" and allow for lots of time in low and no stakes practice when reading.
- Remember that neuroception and threat identification are different for each of us. While we may not identify a threat, students may be having a different experience with different conclusions.
- Notice cues about what nervous system response students might be in.
- Check in with yourself and what state you are currently in.

WHAT DO REGULATED STUDENTS LOOK LIKE?

Self-regulation is a vital life skill that helps students in almost every aspect of their lives, including reading. According to the National Institute for Children's Health Quality, "[S]elf-regulation is the ability for us to manage our thoughts, feelings, and actions. It helps us to remain calm and alert, and supports the capacity to 'respond,' rather than 'react' in the face of our many strong emotions and stressors in life and the environment. . . . Without self-regulation, children struggle to develop meaningful relationships, communicate reciprocally, and succeed at school" (National Institute for Children's Health Quality, 2019).

Self-regulation includes our ability to recognize when we are shifting into a fight, flight, or freeze state and to take actions to shift into a calmer state. It entails our ability to have self-awareness of early signs of dysregulation (hyperarousal or hypoarousal) and to use techniques to help us from becoming dysregulated. We all have physical sensations that let us know our nervous system might become flooded. This may look like feeling hot, having racing thoughts, talking fast, and feeling rushed. This dysregulation is more of a continuum than a box to check. We may be starting to feel dysregulated and still have awareness of it happening on one side, and on the other we may be fully dysregulated without any self-awareness and experiencing a total takeover of our thoughts and rationality.

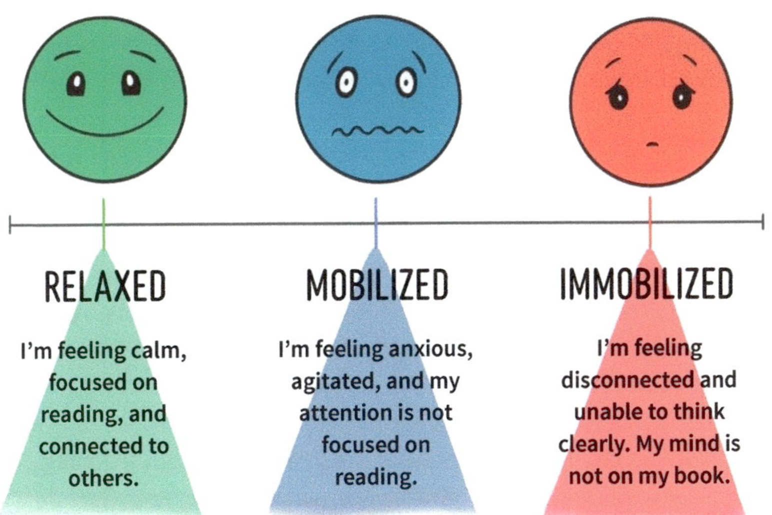

You may want to print this illustration from **https://companion.corwin.com/courses/bodybrainconnection** *(the companion website) for students to have at their desks. They can point to how they are feeling. If you notice many students are not pointing to the relaxed face, you can offer a grounding practice such as calm breathing.*

A LOOK IN THE MIRROR

Self-regulation is not just helpful for students but also for us teachers. We also experience dysregulation when we are triggered by something in our environment. That may look like the constant scanning of the room to make sure all students are on task or glancing up at the clock frequently because there is never enough time to get it all done. Maybe we are still thinking about an interaction with a colleague, administrator, or parent from earlier in the day, or maybe we are dreading the meeting we have later in the afternoon. When we are no longer present in this moment and our minds are stuck in the past or drawn toward the future, we are missing key learning opportunities and also likely feeling some anxiety.

It is totally normal for all of us, especially teachers, to experience challenges. What we do want to be aware of is when we move down the autonomic ladder and are no longer in the window of tolerance. We cannot connect to our students when we are angry and anxious. That may lead to us being less clear with our directions, speaking in an unkind way to a student, being short on patience, and possibly even blaming students for not yet being proficient in the very areas we are there to support them with. When we are feeling safe and secure we would never do those things, but as our nervous system shifts we become less able to make purposeful choices that align with our values.

When we experience prolonged amounts of time in that angry and anxious mode, there comes a point where we shift more, moving further down the ladder into a stuck, hopeless, and disconnected mode. This is when apathy kicks in, we count the minutes until the period or day ends, and we go through the motions, doing just enough to get by. No teacher wants to feel this way and none of us would choose it. We know we are ineffective in our teaching practice and yet because our nervous system is experiencing that "freeze" mode we

The Autonomic Ladder

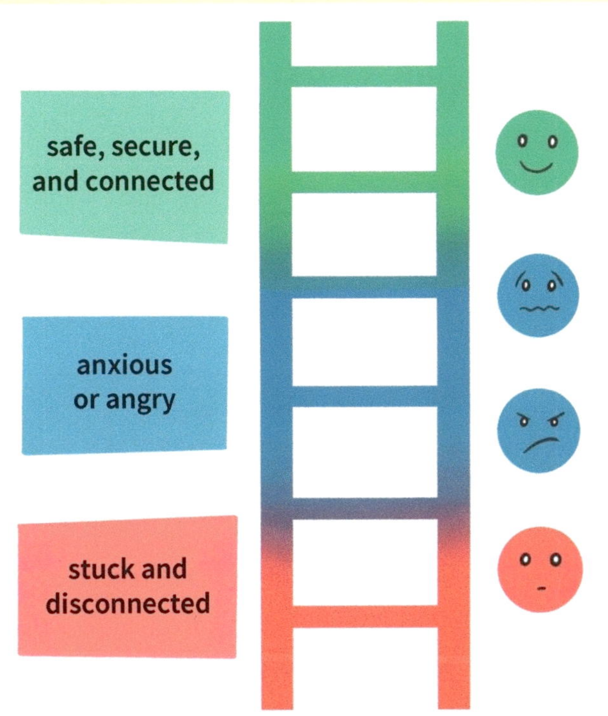

don't always know what to do to shift out of it. We literally cannot think our way into feeling better because our body's nervous system is in control, not our thinking mind.

So what can we do to help ourselves stay regulated and avoid moving down this ladder? First, notice the signs and triggers as soon as possible. If you know that the weekly meeting on Wednesdays causes you anxiety, plan ahead. If you know that the end-of-the-unit assessments and data meetings trigger you, take some time to prepare your body (not just your mind) to feel safe and secure. Begin with self-awareness so you can notice how your body signals to you that you may not be safe. The following self-assessment tool can help.

(Continued)

(Continued)

GETTING TO KNOW MY OWN NERVOUS SYSTEM RESPONSES

Some cues to pay attention to

- *Breath*
- *Heart rate*
- *Body temperature*
- *Body posture*
- *Pace of thoughts*

1. What does it feel like in my body when I feel safe, secure, connected, and in the flow of teaching?
2. What does it feel like in my body when I begin to feel anxiety?
3. What events, time periods, and situations tend to create a feeling of anxiety or anger in my body?
4. What does it feel like in my body when I feel hopeless and disconnected?
5. What events, time periods, and situations tend to create a feeling of hopeless disconnection in my body?

In the pages that follow I offer concrete tools and practices to help all of us, students and teachers, self-regulate. As you read about these practices while thinking about your students, consider which ones may be helpful for you, too. When we are regulated it is helpful for us as teachers and it helps students by offering them a nervous system to co-regulate with.

Students experience regulation when they are in the zone of tolerance, perceive their environment as safe, and can be present in the current context of the classroom. Regulation does not always look the same for all students though. For some students they may benefit from tapping a pencil on their desk or bouncing up and down on their chair in order to self-regulate. I once had a student who regulated by hanging upside down off of an old fabric chair while he read. While at first I was hesitant to let him read this way, I stayed curious and watched a bit. I realized this was the most focused he was and decided it was not bothering anyone else to allow this to happen. He didn't read upside down every day, but many days he did and it did seem to help. As teachers, it can be difficult to watch students fidget, bounce, tap, click, chew, hum, and even dance as they read, because it can be interpreted as silliness or distraction. In many circumstances these physical movements are actually the student's innate self-knowledge kicking in to help them regulate their nervous system. Instead of asking all students to sit still as they read or be silent, consider the following questions:

- What kinds of movements do I see the student making? When?
- What are the impacts of the student's movements?
- Are the movements getting in the way of anyone else's learning?
- What might this physical movement be telling me about this student right now?

When we bring a lens of curiosity, it allows us to let go of our reactions and control and creates space for us to truly meet our students where they are in their bodies.

The benefits of students self-regulating are that they can avoid moving into a nervous system response that puts them into hyperarousal or hypoarousal. They can focus on their learning, take intellectual risks, and engage with peers in conversations about their thinking. Self-regulation can also help other students by offering them a model and a nervous system to co-regulate with.

What do self-regulated students look like? They look like students who are focused on their reading and who can follow along with our teaching and participate in shared reading experiences. They may look calm and still. They may look bouncy and full of energy. They may look away from you as you teach, appearing to be daydreaming. In other words, you can't always tell from looking at a student if they are regulated. One of the key ways to identify who may be regulated and who may not be is to check in with feelings and sensation.

HOW CAN TEACHERS AND STUDENTS CO-REGULATE?

Self-regulation is not something that will automatically develop in all students, but it can be taught through a process called co-regulation. Co-regulation happens when a person is able to show up self-regulated and provide a model and a felt sense of being secure, calm, and in the zone of tolerance themselves. This allows the other person, in this case the student, to regulate themselves based upon their experiences being with a safe and secure adult who helps them feel more safe and secure in their own body. Think of co-regulation in terms of the way a feeling can become "contagious."

Ellen Langer (2024), Harvard professor and bestselling author, wrote about the ways mindfulness is contagious in her book *The Mindful Body*. She cites studies that show that interacting with someone who is mindful increases our own mindfulness. In addition, her research found that when adults are mindful, it increases the collaborative behavior between students and increases engagement.

The **AGILE Approach** to co-regulation, developed by the National Institute for Children's Health Quality, offers a framework for caregivers and teachers to help children co-regulate (Appendix F).

- A - **Affect:** How your tone and expressions convey your emotions. In times of stress, is your affect supportive and calm?
- G - **Gesture:** Facial expressions, hand gestures, body movement, posturing, and pacing all reflect your emotions and are felt by a child during your interactions.
- I - **Intonation:** Modulating the tone of your voice helps convey affect and social/emotional meaning. This is "felt" and "understood" long before words. This communication is stronger than words.
- L - **Latency (Wait):** Wait and give the child time to take in your gestures and intonations. Co-regulation requires patience.
- E - **Engagement:** Before you continue, be sure you have engaged the child. The child's facial expressions, sounds, and body language will tell you if they are engaged.

I can recall childhood sleepovers where one friend would get scared and then all of a sudden all of us were scared too. Or when talking to a friend or family member who is extremely anxious, I begin to feel anxious in my body too. We may also find ourselves gravitating toward a person who we know is sturdy and calm in stressful situations because just being around them helps us feel better. When we find ourselves feeling more regulated by being in the presence of someone else, we are likely experiencing co-regulation. Of course we can offer students a feeling of safety in our words, but when our nervous systems are regulated it offers a much more potent sense of safety that can reach their nervous systems.

What does co-regulation feel like in a classroom? When you are feeling calm and connected in your own body, your body language communicates a feeling of safety. Students may be watching your cues, getting in sync with your breathing, and noticing how your posture, tone of voice, and gestures communicate a sense of connection and calm. As your self-regulation remains consistent, students begin to feel calmer in their own bodies. It may take a few minutes, but they eventually pick up the book, begin reading, and may even ask for help to get started.

Sometimes students feel embarrassed after returning to a regulated state because they are aware that they acted in ways that they would not have chosen when they were dysregulated. If they argued, got angry, or drew attention to themselves for other negatively perceived actions, they may need some time and positive communication to reengage with social interactions. When we teachers normalize getting dysregulated and model how to reconnect and repair, it shows students how to do the same.

Some ways to model reconnection include the following:

- Taking a cleansing exhale and saying, “Time for a fresh start.”
- Naming the shift in our feelings with words like “It seems we are feeling calmer now and ready to begin.”
- Acknowledging struggle and creating space to move on. We might say, “That was hard. It is OK for things to feel hard and for feelings to get big. Now that we feel calmer, we are ready to get into our reading.”

(Continued)

(Continued)

- Using humor to defuse tension. The humor should never be at a student's expense. Sometimes a quick joke and laughter can shift the feeling to more lightness.
- Letting students know we are not carrying a grudge or judgment after big feelings are expressed. That may sound like, "Sometimes our emotions take over and after we let them out we feel better. This happens to everyone. Let's move forward together."

WHAT TECHNIQUES REDUCE ANXIETY AND SUPPORT A SENSE OF SAFETY?

Now that we understand what is happening in our nervous systems and why, we can begin to focus on how to support students. The following pages offer ways to reduce anxiety and help students get a felt sense of safety in their bodies. I know it can be tempting and time efficient to just tell them with our words that they don't need to feel anxious, but we now understand that when we perceive something as a threat, our nervous system goes through a response process that literally prevents our words from making a difference. We need to communicate to our students' nervous systems, and that happens by working with the body.

There are a few things to know before engaging in the whole body practices that follow.

- First, this does not need to take a large amount of instructional time, and it costs no money. With just thirty seconds to three minutes you can help students get a felt sense of safety and prime them for less anxiety.
- Second, the practices in this section are research- and evidence-based. Neuroscientists, psychologists, social workers, medical doctors, and researchers from a variety of fields have discovered ways to reduce anxiety and handle stress.
- Third, all of the practices can help you as well as your students. If you devote a minute or two each day to grounding practices that help students, you might as well do them at the same time. When you model the practices, you help students take them more seriously and it also helps you feel more regulated in your own body too.

- Finally, these practices can be done in any order and you don't need to do them all. Experiment with each one and find the ones that work for your students and for you.

When to Incorporate Grounding Practices

It is extremely likely that at least one and often several students in your class are experiencing anxiety or perceiving reading as a threat. It is helpful to be proactive and assume that someone in the classroom would benefit from a grounding practice each day. For this reason, taking the first minute of class to incorporate a whole group practice that can help students feel safe and secure and avoid moving down the autonomic nervous system is a good use of time. By making a grounding practice a daily routine that helps students transition into work time, you are setting up students to be successful and more present for your teaching and their learning.

Of course you can also lead students in additional practice in small groups as needed. These small groups could be preplanned or, more likely in the moment, responsive groups based on what you are noticing during class time. While it does take a few minutes to call over students to the small group area and lead them through a breathing exercise, it is time well spent if it helps them regulate and then focus on reading for the remainder of the period.

It's Not About the Anxiety Content

After reading the pages leading up to this part of the chapter you may be wondering about specific aspects of reading that may be triggering anxiety and fear in students. What about the student who struggled so much with learning to decode that even looking at words sends them into a dysregulated state? What about the student who cheers for the whole class read-aloud but then does everything they can to avoid having to read independently? What about the student who still gets hot and then dissociates when asked to read in front of their peers?

Students bring their past experiences and triggers with them into the classroom, and they may be connected to many different aspects of the reading process. The good news is that we don't have to address each student's fear and anxiety differently. When nervous systems are having a response to reading, we don't need to address the content that triggers it; rather, we need to address the body, the nervous system. So, using a breathing technique *before* reading can help all of the students who experience anxiety, no matter the cause. The breathing technique is not harming the students who don't experience anxiety about reading, but it is essential that students are never forced to participate if they choose not to. Everyone gets the opportunity to feel grounded, secure, and connected, and that helps all of the students focus more on the text in their hands.

Grounding Practices

Each of the following practices (beginning on page 56) is meant to be done before anxiety kicks in. Think of that autonomic ladder metaphor. When students are about to begin a reading experience, you want them to be on that top rung in a calm and securely connected state. In order to remain there they may need to tell their nervous system they are safe. This communication is not done in words but in their bodies. Taking a minute to prime the nervous system for safety is worthwhile as it helps students regulate their emotions and sets their brains up to be ready to think, read, and discuss. Of course, any time during the day, as anxiety creeps in, students can use these grounding practices on their own, oftentimes without their peers even knowing they are doing it. The goal is not just that they use these practices when prompted by you but also as needed when they feel they need it.

Many of the practices in this section are evidence-based practices that fall under the larger umbrella term of *mindfulness-based stress reduction* (MBSR), developed by Jon Kabat-Zinn. These practices have a robust research backing in both qualitative and quantitative studies. Grounding experiences that are part of the MBSR framework have been shown to do the following:

- Increase interoception, the awareness of one's own internal state (Damasio, 2003; de Jong et al., 2016; Farb et al., 2007; Fissler et al., 2016)
- Develop emotional awareness (Hölzel et al., 2011)
- Lead to gains in attention (Bornemann et al., 2015; Erwin & Robinson, 2016)
- Help with self-regulation (Brown & Ryan, 2003; Lakey et al., 2008)
- Develop more resilience to stress (Zenner et al., 2014)
- Lead to a calmer nervous system (parasympathetic nervous system) (O. G. Cameron, 2001; Ditto et al., 2006)

Take a few minutes to check in with your nervous system. Jot down what you notice about yourself and your students.

BODY SCAN (Appendix G)

When: at the very start of class or the start of a reading experience, anytime you transition

Time frame: 1–3 minutes

Steps:

> A body scan practice is positively and significantly correlated with decreased anxiety and increased non-reactivity.
> (Carmody & Baer, 2008)

1. Tell students they are going to have one minute to set their bodies up for learning.
2. Explain that we are not judging our sensations and our job is to simply notice them. There are no wrong sensations and we are not trying to change anything.
3. Ask students to sit up with their feet planted firmly on the ground. Take an intentional inhale and exhale through the nose. Invite students to close their eyes or bring their gaze down to the floor if they are not comfortable closing their eyes completely.

4. Starting at the feet, invite students to pay attention to what they are feeling in their bodies. Move awareness up the body from the feet, legs, abdomen, chest, arms, shoulders, and face. End by having students feel the contact their feet are making on the ground.
5. Give students a few seconds to sit in silence before ending the experience.

Tips:

- End by asking students to open their eyes and then you can begin teaching. Talking about the sensations may lead to distractions and comparisons and is not necessary.
- Use age-appropriate language so that older students don't feel uncomfortable with the terminology. Yes, there may be giggles at first when you ask them to feel sensations in their bodies, but if you give them a few days of practice the awkwardness should go away. For teens who would balk at anything called a "body scan," you can use more scientific terminology like *interoception*.
- Remind students they can use their breath to relax into any areas that feel tight as they scan. They don't have to do anything, but they can let go of tension.
- After leading students through the scan a few times with success, you can let them do a self-guided body scan. This means instead of telling them what to sense, the students go through the process on their own at their own pace.

The following script is adapted from the Greater Good Science Center (n.d.).

> Begin by bringing your attention into your body.
> You can close your eyes or bring your gaze down to the floor.
> Feel the weight of your body on the chair.
> Take a few deep and slow breaths.
> Notice your feet on the floor. Feel the weight and pressure, vibration, and heat.
> Notice your legs against the chair. Feel the pressure, pulsing, heaviness, or lightness.
> Notice your back against the chair.
> Bring your attention into your stomach. If your stomach is tight, let it soften.
> Take a breath.
> Notice your hands. If your hands are tight, allow them to soften.
> Feel any sensation in your arms. Let your shoulders be soft.
> Notice your neck and throat. Let them be soft. Relax.
> Soften your jaw. Let your face and facial muscles be soft.

CALM BREATHING (Appendix H)

When: at the very start of class or the start of a reading experience, anytime you transition

Time frame: 1–2 minutes

Steps:

1. Sit up tall with your feet on the floor. Let your arms relax down at your sides.
2. Close your eyes or bring your gaze down to the floor.
3. Slowly breathe in through your nose. Notice your chest filling up with air and your belly expanding.
4. Now slowly breathe out through your nose. Notice your chest emptying and your belly relaxing.
5. Repeat this breathing pattern a few more times.
6. End by returning to your normal breath and noticing how you feel.

"Mindfulness breathing meditation has an impact on reducing stress and anxiety in students."

(Komariah et al., 2022)

Tips:

- You can add a count to the breath, starting with inhaling for two and exhaling for two. Build up to the count of four if students are ready.
- Elongating the exhale for a longer count helps you relax. When the body is holding onto a bit of carbon dioxide it becomes a natural sedative (Han et al., 2023). Invite students who are already comfortable with the breathing exercises to briefly hold their inhalation and then slowly exhale for a few counts longer than they inhaled.
- Make sure that if any student feels dizzy or lightheaded, they stop the exercise and take their time before getting up.
- Always check to make sure students are physically well enough to participate in intentional breathing exercises before inviting them to try.

SENSORY NOTICING (5-4-3-2-1) (Appendix I)

When: at the very start of class or the start of a reading experience, anytime you transition

Time frame: 1–2 minutes

Steps:

> "This gesture of awareness opens us up to the possibility of acting at least a bit more wisely in this world."
> (Kabat-Zinn, 2021)

1. Acknowledge FIVE things you see around you. It could be a chart, a spot on the wall, your teacher's earrings, etc.
2. Acknowledge FOUR things you can touch around you. It could be the metal leg on your chair, the texture of your sweater, or the ground under your feet, etc.

3. Acknowledge THREE things you hear outside your body. This could be students talking in the hallway, a bird chirping outside, yourself tapping your pencil on the desk, etc.
4. Acknowledge TWO things you can smell. This could be the pencil shavings, the lotion on your hands, or someone's rotten apple peel in the garbage, etc.
5. Acknowledge ONE thing you can taste. What does the inside of your mouth taste like? This could be gum, peanut butter from your lunch, or staleness from thirst, etc.

Tips:

- You don't always have to do all five steps. Just taking a moment to have a sensory experience brings us out of our thoughts and into our bodies and environment.
- If students enjoy this practice, try bringing in a candle or playing soft music to include a few more sensory experiences. Just be aware that some scents and sounds are too strong for students, so err on the side of subtle.
- The listening sensory experience on its own can be helpful to create calm in the classroom. Dim the lights, allow students to put their heads down, and then guide them to listen for sounds. They can move from sounds very close to them and try to move their sense of sound out more to the classroom, hallway, outside, etc. How far can they hear?

VISUALIZING PERSONAL POWER (Appendix J)

When: at the very start of class or the start of a reading experience, anytime you transition

Time frame: 30 seconds to 1 minute

Steps:

1. Sit in a comfortable position and close your eyes.
2. Think of a time in your life when you felt personally powerful.
3. Picture the moment. Make a clear movie in your mind of what you were doing and how you felt.
4. Take in that feeling of personal power.

"When we feel personally powerful, we not only show up, but we show up as both strong and generous, as both confident and kind."

(Cuddy, 2015)

Tips:

- Dr. Amy Cuddy found that a sense of personal power is different from social power. Social power is the ability to control the actions of others, and personal power is our ability to control our own states and actions. This practice is focused on personal power, so make sure students understand the difference.
- When visualizing and feeling into our own personal power, we are priming ourselves to feel more personally powerful and confident for what's coming next. In this way we set ourselves up to feel ready for the next challenge, like reading a new book or learning a new strategy.
- The moment we are picturing does not have to be connected to school or reading. It is not about the content of the moment we are visualizing but is about the feeling associated with it.

LAUGHTER YOGA (Appendix K)

When: at the end of class or reading time, anytime you transition, when students are feeling anxious and need a fresh start to relieve tension

Time frame: 30 seconds to 1 minute

Steps:

1. Stand up and spread out.
2. Begin by clapping rhythmically 1-2, 1-2-3.
3. Add in the sounds "ho-ho, ha-ha-ha" as you clap.
4. Pick up the pace as you go.
5. Drop the clapping and just make the sounds "ho-ho, ha-ha-ha." Possibly add in other gestures like hands up and down.
6. Let yourself smile, move, make eye contact, and connect with one another.
7. A more spontaneous laughter will likely occur. Let that happen.
8. End with a closing routine, such as getting quieter with our voices and doing a long exhalation, before sitting back down.

"Scientific studies have shown that there is an increase in serotonin and dopamine with laughter yoga."

(Laughter Yoga International: Laughteryoga.org)

Tips:

- According to Langer (2024), joy is a way to create regulation in our bodies. When students are joyfully laughing, they are not just reducing anxiety but also creating regulated nervous systems. If students are feeling grumpy, discouraged, and anxious, consider a laughter yoga exercise. Or be proactive and start with one before the period begins.
- Laughing releases endorphins and "happy" hormones like dopamine and serotonin. The release of these hormones is a safe way to help students regulate. And by doing the laughter together, you are co-regulating off of one another. If you have a particularly silly class, you can harness their need for laughter with an intentional exercise.
- Don't assume students (of any age) will know how to transition from laughter yoga to the next activity. For this reason, choose laughter yoga after reading as a way to recharge and begin the next learning experience. Teach them how to end the laughing session with a routine that clearly shows you are moving on to the next part of the day. Some ideas for endings include high five a neighbor, sit and feel, or big exhale and jump. After the final action students can practice sitting and being ready to learn again.

SOME VARIATIONS OF LAUGHTER YOGA (KANIGEL, 2021)

Lion laughter: Stick out your tongue, open your eyes wide, and stretch your hands out like claws while laughing.

Humming laughter: Laugh with the mouth closed and hum.

Silent laughter: Open your mouth wide and laugh without making a sound.

Gradient laughter: Start by smiling and then slowly begin to chuckle softly. Increase the intensity of the laugh until you've achieved a hearty laugh. Then gradually bring the laugh down to a smile again. Bonus: this can be an opportunity to teach some vocabulary words if you put the words up on the board as you guide students through the gradient.

Smile	Chuckle	Giggle	Guffaw	Roar

A SUMMARY OF KEY IDEAS FROM CHAPTER 3

In this chapter we examined what anxiety may look and feel like and how it impacts students. We learned about the autonomic nervous system and its role in regulation. By including grounding practices, we can proactively support all students, especially the ones who experience stress and would benefit from more co-regulation.

- It is important for students to experience safety in their bodies so that learning can happen.
- Sometimes what seems like distractibility, lack of focus, and "misbehavior" may really be dysregulation and signal to us teachers that the student is experiencing fight, flight, or freeze responses.
- Our bodies use neuroception to scan the environment on an unconscious level for potential threats. This neuroception is tied to the vagus nerve and our autonomic nervous system. We can feel safe and secure (ventral vagal response), shut down and disconnected (dorsal vagal response), or anxious and angry (sympathetic response).
- We cannot think our way out of hyperarousal or hypoarousal. We can co-regulate our bodies with others to shift our nervous system into the zone of tolerance.
- By focusing on grounding practices with all students, we can create the context for more self-regulation and co-regulation to happen before students become dysregulated.
- Our bodies' autonomic nervous system works the same way as our students and the practices in this section also can help us.

A SUMMARY OF PRACTICES FROM CHAPTER 3

Practices	Reflection Questions	When and Where I May Use This
Track your own nervous system with the autonomic ladder (see page 47).	How am I feeling right now? What might my body need to feel safe and secure?	
Acknowledge the ways students may be experiencing learning threats. Make a class chart like the one on page 40 and discuss these feelings with students.	Which of these experiences can you relate to? How do you know when you are experiencing these feelings? What do these feel like in your body?	
Explain the three autonomic nervous system states to students. Use the image on page 45 as a self-reflection tool for students.	What does the "zone of tolerance" feel like to you? What helps you widen your zone of tolerance?	
Track character feeling states using the autonomic ladder.	How is the character feeling? Where are they on the ladder? What connections can I make to this character?	
Use the AGILE co-regulation approach (page 50).	Which elements of this approach can I focus more on? What might this approach look and sound like that feels authentic to my teaching style?	

(Continued)

(Continued)

Practices	Reflection Questions	When and Where I May Use This
Repair and reconnect after dysregulated behaviors (page 51).	What kind of restart and repair would help this relationship? How can I turn this into a learning experience and build more connections with the student?	
Lead the grounding practice called Body Scan (page 56).	How can I introduce this to students in ways that acknowledge it can be awkward to feel our bodily sensations but also helpful?	
Lead the grounding practice called Calm Breathing (page 58).	When might I work calm breathing into the class period? How can I remember to scaffold students to use this practice on their own as needed?	
Lead the grounding practice called Sensory Noticing (page 60).	How might students with different sensory needs respond to this practice?	
Lead the grounding practice called Visualize Personal Power (page 62).	How can I help students understand the concept of personal power and experience it in their bodies?	
Lead the grounding practice called Laughter Yoga (page 64).	Who in my class might really benefit from this joyful experience?	

Chapter 4

Students' Bodies Help Them Handle Difficulty

"The mind, once stretched by a new idea, never returns to its original dimensions."

— Ralph Waldo Emerson

PRIME YOURSELF

As you begin to read this section, expect to lose focus around page 91, which is about two-thirds of the way through. If you don't want this to happen, there are a few ways to prime your expectations to support your performance.

First, tell yourself you will read two chapters today, and then give yourself a break after the first one. This will trick your body into not experiencing fatigue until you have finished reading the entire chapter.

Second, turn away from all watches and clocks. Don't look at the time and, if possible, don't pause to look at the clock as you read.

Third, find someone to talk to about your reading and, if possible, ask them to join you as you read. Meet up somewhere cozy and read side by side, or at the very least meet up over coffee to talk about it.

We tend to think about students' ability to focus, handle challenges, and pay attention as choices they make or as innate abilities that some are lucky enough to be born with. Research has shown us that our bodies have a much bigger impact than we tend to think when it comes to stamina, perseverance, and performance. As you begin this section, notice how your own attention wanes and when. Notice how your body responds when you're confronted with ideas that don't match what you already think.

This chapter focuses on the very real ways our brain's expectations and our body's experiences impact performance. This means that it is not just innate strengths and application of strategies that leads to focus, perseverance, and the ability to pay attention as we learn. Some key building blocks of being a reader across subject areas include the ability to

- read with stamina,
- develop confidence to handle challenges,
- productively work through struggle,
- stay motivated,
- pay close attention, and
- experience reading as fun.

As educators, many of us may have assumed these building blocks were gifted to a few students, maybe fewer each year, and that the rest of the students will need to be pulled along with coaxing.

It can feel so overwhelming when students enter the classroom without the ability to focus their attention and the apparent unwillingness to persevere through difficulty and put the work in. On our most exhausted days we may even blame students and call them "lazy" or "checked out" for not seeming to care enough or put enough effort in. The issue with resorting to these sorts of labels and beliefs is that it doesn't help us feel any better, it can make us feel completely disempowered to make an impact, and it is sensed by our students, who can feel our judgments.

In this chapter we will learn how important body-brain connections are and how they impact all of these building blocks of being a reader across content areas. My hope is that as you read this section you will learn new ways of viewing students' performance, feel hopeful and curious about other ways of looking at students' experiences, and then take action by trying out new ideas.

HOW CAN BODY AND BRAIN CONNECTIONS HELP WITH STAMINA?

Ms. Thomas sits on a stool by the rug while her students lean in listening to her read aloud the second chapter of *A Rover's Story,* by Jasmine Warga. Most of the students have wide open eyes and laser-like focus on the story. They can't wait to hear more from the narrators who happen to be a Mars rover and a young girl. Since the chapters are short, Ms. Thomas plans to read both Chapters 2 and 3 today and then open up a discussion with students about what they think about the characters. About halfway through the third chapter, Ms. Thomas notices a few students begin to wiggle around. Their eyes are scanning the room and are not so laser focused anymore. Mia begins to pat the back of the student in front of her. That student, Olivia, gets distracted and turns around to tell Mia to stop touching her. Ms. Thomas tries to redirect the class back to the book, but she finds herself stopping every few sentences to get the class's attention. She's wondering why they can't just stay focused for a few more minutes; after all, they seemed to be enjoying the book just a few minutes ago.

After many of her seventh period students did not do the reading at home, Ms. Williams decided to ask her students why they were behind. They explained that they had so many activities and jobs to do after school that by the time they got home and ate something, took a shower, and then sat down to read, they were exhausted. They explained that they really did want to read at home but there was little space to really give it the attention needed. So, Ms. Williams decided to use today's class period for in-class reading so that students could both catch up and also get reconnected and hopefully hooked back into the book. Students began reading quietly and then about fifteen minutes later they seemed to lose focus one by one. First the students by the window seemed to be watching the birds on the tree. Then the students by the door seemed to be noticing everyone who was walking by. Even her own focus drifted to a meeting she had after school. She wondered why everyone's stamina seemed to wane and what she could do to help.

Students like the ones in Ms. Thomas's and Ms. William's classes are not unusual. They begin the reading experience focused and then over time their minds wander, their attention wanes, and they end up wasting the latter part of the class or period. The typical way of interpreting the issue is that students lack stamina for staying focused and lack perseverance for working for extended periods of time. But, research from Harvard professor Ellen Langer points us in a different direction. Rather than be frustrated by students' lack of stamina and focus, we can better understand what might be going on and make some adjustments to our assumptions and our classroom practices.

Let's consider the research on stamina as a way to look at why and how some students are able to read for large chunks of time and why others tend to lose focus almost immediately. Langer's (2009) research from her book *Counterclockwise* found that fatigue, which is what gets in the way of stamina, is based on the way we structure time. She claims that "mental and physical energy are not governed by different underlying processes" (Langer, 2024, p. 123). Our perception of fatigue occurs based on how far into an activity we get, not the actual amount of time we spend doing it.

In one study of fatigue, Langer's research team asked college students to do either one hundred or two hundred jumping jacks depending on the group they were put in. They were asked to self-report when they got tired. They found that both groups experienced fatigue about two-thirds of the way through the jumping jacks—the first group around 65 to 70 jumps and the second group around 130 to 140 jumps.

This study was replicated with typing. This time the researchers looked at when the typist started to make errors (as a sign of fatigue). Again, they found they didn't appear until around two-thirds of the way through, no matter if they were in a group typing one page or two pages. As a result of these two studies, the research team replicated the tests several times and they found that fatigue is a mental construct that has physical impacts (Langer, 2024).

The findings of these studies led the researchers to conclude that we impose a structure on tasks to make sure they have a beginning, middle, and end. Then, when we shift from the middle to the end, we experience fatigue. It is not the number of minutes we read in total but the shift from the middle to the end where we get tired and lose our focus and stamina. This fatigue construct is based on the person knowing how long or how much they would be asked to do. "Fatigue depended on how long they expected" the task to be (Langer, 2024, p. 125). This has implications for students' reading, listening, and writing stamina in and out of the classrooms.

"The idea of structuring the tasks we do with a clear beginning, middle, and end serves a purpose. . . . Knowing that we essentially control when we get tired can enable us to willfully change when doing so is to our advantage" (Langer, 2024, p. 127). As teachers, we can help students read, write, and listen for longer periods of time by knowing they will lose focus around two-thirds of the way through. So if we want students to read for twenty minutes, we can tell them they will be reading for thirty minutes, knowing that at the twenty-minute mark they will likely need the break.

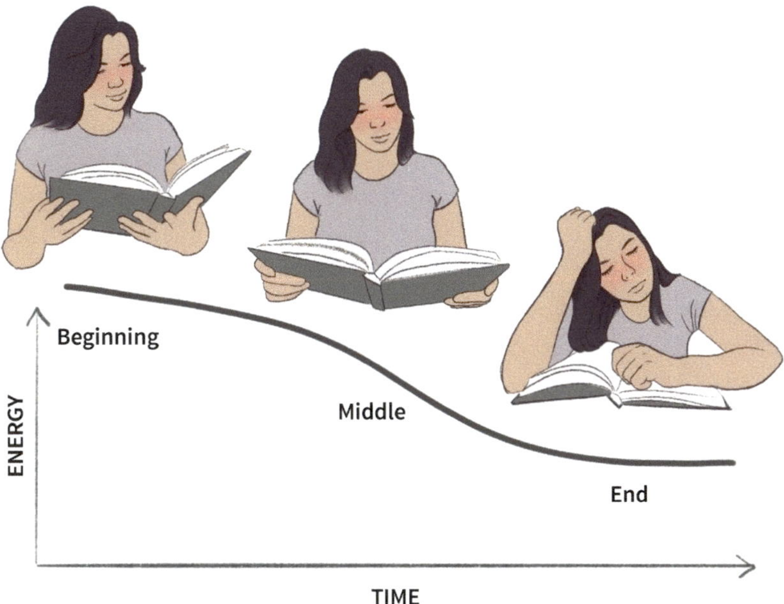

Expect fatigue to set in as you shift from the middle to the end of a task like reading. Explain this concept to students so they are prepared and ready to refocus as needed.

Fatigue may be constructed in our minds as a beginning, middle, and end, but it is experienced, felt, and witnessed in our bodies. There are some elements of fatigue we can see, like yawning, error making, head bobbing, and eyes drooping. We've all been on the end of teaching when we watched a student struggle to stay alert and maybe even awake. Fatigue also shows up as slow breathing, mind wandering, and lower heart rate. While this sluggish body feeling can be due to physical conditions like low blood sugar, it is also likely due to perception of time and the expectation of being tired.

Langer's research team found "perceived time was more important that real time" (Langer, 2024, p. 154) in a study of people with type 2 diabetes. The participants were told the study they were participating in was about the role of blood sugar in cognitive functioning. Their blood sugar was tested, and then they were told to play a video game. Every fifteen minutes they were told to shift to a new video game. One of the groups of people with diabetes looked at a clock that listed real time, one group had a clock that ran twice as fast as real time, and one group had a clock that ran half as fast as real time. Then the participants' blood sugar was tested again. It was not the actual time that had passed but the perception of elapsed time that impacted the blood sugar levels, even after controlling for things like interest level and stress level.

These studies show us that it is not always how many minutes we do something that leads to fatigue in our bodies but how long *we think* we are doing something. This also led researchers to conclude that physical symptoms of fatigue may originate in our brains, not our bodies. As teachers, we can observe students to notice when fatigue is setting in. We can also invite students to pay attention to their own bodies and minds and to notice the subtle and not so subtle signs of fatigue.

What Fatigue May Look and Feel Like in Students

Type	Examples
Mental	I am no longer aware of what I am doing and I am "zoned out." I can't remember what I was just reading about. I'm thinking about something that has nothing to do with what I am doing right now.
Physical	I can't keep my eyes open. My hand hurts and I need to shake it out. My shoulders are slumped and I want to put my head down.
Social	I can only think about myself and my needs right now. I haven't really been listening to what you just said. I really want space to be by myself for a bit.

Time Management Considerations and the Two-Thirds Rule

When designing lessons, it is important to consider the two-thirds rule for fatigue. We know that if you have a forty-five minute period, then thirty minutes in, students will likely get tired. This is not their fault; rather, it is due to the construct of time and how students' expectations shape it. For the next few days, spend some time looking for and noticing when students seem to experience fatigue. Jot down when in the period you noticed it and what they were doing. Then use your observational data to make some shifts.

There are a few ways to "hack" this two-thirds rule or at least plan with it in mind.

- Plan in a break two-thirds of the way through.
- Hide your clocks so students don't know how long they have been working. (Or in some places, don't ask them to fix that broken clock on your wall.)
- Plan for more collaborative and reflective work at the two-thirds mark when students will need a shift from independent work to something else.
- Flip the order of the classroom experiences so the final third of the class is not always the same. End with reading some days, end with talking some days, end with instruction on other days. This will ensure students don't always lose stamina for the same experiences, and it also keeps some novelty in the classroom.
- Teach students the two-thirds rule. Let them know to expect fatigue and focus drops at that point and to plan accordingly.

HOW CAN STUDENTS' BODIES HELP THEM HANDLE DIFFICULTY?

Now that we know that fatigue and the physical manifestations of it are caused by our perception of time, we can also consider how students perceive difficulty. In other words, why do some students think reading is hard and others do not. We could simply say that the one student is a more fluent reader so they would think it was easier. That may be the case. But, what if there were other factors that contribute to our sense of how challenging something like a learning task actually is? And how can we support students who feel daunted by classroom learning experiences and often get too intimidated to even begin on their own? We can tell our students they can do it and to believe in themselves, but often our words aren't going to help them literally see the task as less challenging. Research studies have shown that a few key factors impact our expectations and therefore our ability to handle difficulty.

- Support from others makes challenges seem less difficult.
- Changing the sequence of experiences enables us to succeed in more challenging tasks.

Supportive Presence

Achor (2018) brought my attention to a surprising study when he discussed it in his book *Big Potential*. Researchers brought participants to the bottom of a mountain and asked them to estimate the steepness. In previous research studies people tend to overestimate steepness when standing on their own at the base of a mountain (Burrow et al., 2016). Being on their own led people to overestimate the challenge. In this study researchers had participants stand and estimate the steepness while standing next to a trusted friend (Schnall et al., 2008). "The researchers found that if you are looking at a hill and judging how steep it is, the mere presence of social support around you transforms your perception. In fact, if you look at a hill while standing next to someone you consider to be a friend, the hill looks ten to twenty percent less steep than if you were facing that hill alone" (Achor, 2018, p. 31). Even when the trusted friend was three feet away, facing a different direction and staying silent, the results held true. This led the researchers to conclude that our perception is impacted by and resourced by the support of others and not an objective truth. As Achor (2018) explains, "So, mentally and physically, mountains seem more climbable, successes more achievable, and obstacles more surmountable with others beside us" (p. 31).

Show an image like this or a photo of a steep mountain to students. Explain how having a supportive friend or teacher by their side helps them feel less overwhelmed.

Although our students are not staring up at mountains in our classrooms, they are holding a text in their hands and having a perception of how difficult it will be to read, understand, and discuss it. When students have trusted peers and solid relationships with their teachers, believing their teacher is someone they can trust for support, they are more likely to perceive the text and task to be less challenging and more doable. The "steepness" of the learning experience will be judged to be less difficult because of the social support that the people around them provide. This is just one reason why having positive and supportive relationships in classrooms is not a luxury or fad but a necessity when it comes to helping students work through challenges and feel confident enough they can in fact begin. Teach students about the power of trusted relationships with friends and teachers and use the following list of practices to make this research finding more concrete for students.

The steepness of the learning "hill" can be minimized by

- thinking of a person who is supportive and how you can rely on them,
- thinking back to a time when you felt personally powerful and able to handle challenges,
- previewing the challenge with a supportive peer or teacher, or
- sitting next to a supportive peer or teacher while you take on the challenge.

The Power of Peer Partnerships

Now that we know that the presence of a trusted person can help us view texts and tasks as a little less challenging, we can think about how we can use this information in our classrooms. Most of us already incorporate some form of peer collaboration to likely very mixed results. We can reconsider who gets paired up, why, and in what capacity. First, I would explain the supportive presence research to students so they understand the role they are playing and the importance of the work they do by just being there for their partners. Then, you can model for students how to communicate supportive presence for one another (Appendix L).

WAYS TO BE A SUPPORTIVE PARTNER

- Smile.
- Lean in.
- Nod your head.
- Use positive language such as "I believe you can do it."
- Give them space to do the work themselves.
- Mirror back what you are seeing them do to honor their efforts.

Use a chart like this one to teach students how to be a supportive partner. They can also use it to reflect and set goals for next steps as partners.

Oftentimes teachers consider whether students who are good friends outside of class should be paired up in class. Of course, the answer to that question is "it depends." But, from the perspective of the supportive presence research, it would be helpful to pair up students who trust one another when the goal of the partnership is to help one another work through something challenging. Putting students who do not trust one another or who do not get along together might be the right choice if you are going to be there with them and help them reconnect and work through interpersonal issues, but for most students, having a friend next to them can really help when reading something complex, when analyzing a text, or when developing the skill to not give up when it gets hard.

A LOOK IN THE MIRROR

I still remember squeezing my best friend's hand right before jumping into the lake for our first ever triathlon and believing it was doable at that moment. If she had not been there with me, I would have been so much more scared and been really questioning if I could actually do it. Her presence did not take my nerves away or literally make the swim, bike, or run easier, but it did make my perception of how hard it would be a little less.

Think about a time in your life that something was a challenge but you had someone you trusted there with you.

- Picture that moment in your mind.
- What were you feeling? Thinking?
- What did you believe?
- How did that person's presence impact you?
- What did support feel like?

Many days as teachers we feel like we are looking up at mountains. Who do you have in your professional life that can stand next to you and help you perceive the steepness as a little bit less? Our colleagues can be more than thinking partners and also serve as that trusted friend who literally helps us see the work we do as a little less challenging. That "little less" can have a big impact on how we think and what we do.

Change the Sequence

Another factor that impacts learning is the sequencing of experiences. In order to test whether the order of tasks impacted performance, Langer's (2024) research team used eye exam tests to show people that "seeing the body as separate from the mind encourages the belief in set limits for our senses" (p. 129). Her research found that believing that our sensory experiences are not fixed, but rather impacted by our expectations and contexts, helped people successfully complete more difficult tasks.

Studies with eye charts showed that changing the sequence of tasks allowed participants to be able to literally see better. Typical eye exam charts start with larger print on top and then the letters get progressively smaller, setting the expectation that at some point the type will be too small to see. In one study, researchers changed the chart so that the smaller type was on top and the letters got progressively larger. This was done to reverse the expectation the participants had. They found that people could read the smaller print lines that came first when they shifted the person's expectation. They literally scored higher on the eye exam and their vision "improved."

In another study, they had people use the typical eye exam chart, but they had them start two-thirds of the way down, where the print was already quite small. By starting there, instead of at the top, participants were more likely to be able to read the smallest print. These were the same participants who could not see the smallest lines when they began all the way at the top. Again, their vision "improved" by changing the sequence of where they started.

Because Langer's group didn't want to just study visual sensory perception, they conducted another study on listening. Four groups of participants were given a hearing test and then were asked to listen to a podcast. Each group received different information prior to listening. In one group they were told that listening to the podcast would improve their hearing. The second group was told to listen to the podcast with no additional information. The third group was told that by listening at a low volume it would lead to hearing improvement. The fourth group listened to the podcast at a low volume but was not given any information about why the volume was low. All of the groups listened to a podcast, two groups were primed to expect improvement in hearing, two groups listened at low volume. The results showed that listening to the low volume led to the most hearing improvement regardless of whether they were given an explanation about why ahead of time. Put another way, by listening at a lower volume, it made the task more difficult and also led to better results. This study helped them support their findings from the vision test that "making the task harder did indeed make it easier at the next attempt" (Langer, 2024, p. 131).

The implications of these studies on classroom instruction can help us rethink the ways we tend to sequence our curriculum and our instructional experiences. Traditionally we tend to start with the easier tasks and work our way to more complex concepts and texts. This makes sense when we think about learning as a brain only based activity where concepts need to be stacked on top of each other in an incremental way. If we consider Langer's research, we might try to shift the sequence of difficulty, starting with more complex and challenging tasks first. Of course that doesn't mean putting Shakespeare in front of second graders. We still want to be aware of developmental appropriateness, but there are ways in which the sequence within the developmental expectations of our grade/course could be shifted.

One example of shifting the sequence where students do more complex thinking before less complex thinking is with close reading. Oftentimes students can interpret themes on earlier reads and then go back on later rereads to identify evidence for that thinking. By beginning with the complex, more challenging task of interpretation, students can then go back and work on finding specific parts of the text, an often less difficult task because the words are right in the text. (For a sample lesson where the sequence was shifted see Appendix M.)

Ways to Shift the Sequence of Learning Experiences

Type	Example
Text shift	Start with a complex text and then work toward simpler texts focused on the same topic, theme, or skill. (See Appendix M for a sample lesson idea.)
Teaching shift	End with whole class teaching instead of starting with it. Start with independent work and then base your teaching on what students need support with.
Focus shift	Set students up to do more interpretive and analytic work right away with a text. Later, move to more in-text work.

Change the Language

Another shift we can consider based on Langer's research is how expectations are shaped by our language choices and framing of tasks. Think of the ways we prime students before learning experiences with our directions and language choices. We have a lot of influence on how perceptions are shaped. Be aware of how we describe a text as hard or challenging or "above grade level" and how students respond to this framing. We also can be more aware of what we tell them, if anything, before they take on a challenge about what the impacts will be. For example, do we say, "The time you spend reading this challenging poem will help you be able to read other figurative texts more easily." If we frame it this way, we are not just telling them our "why" but also setting up an expectation for students that this will be hard. All of our messages and directions prime expectations, and we can benefit from being more intentional in our language choices. Ask yourself, "Does it help students to know I think this is hard?" If not, keep that to yourself and let them work through it. They may surprise you.

HOW CAN WE SUPPORT STUDENT MOTIVATION?

As I read the research on perception of difficulty I wondered about the role that someone's motivation played in their willingness to work through challenges. Was motivation simply reverse engineered with task design, by bringing in a supportive presence and changing the sequence? Langer (2024) found that "we prefer a challenge to guaranteed success. It's the struggle that is fun" (p. 201). She uses examples such as when you are newly learning the game tic-tac-toe it is fun until you figure out how to win every time. Or how hitting the elevator button as a young child, barely tall enough to reach it, brought joy. Now, as an adult, you likely never feel joy when hitting an elevator button. The novelty of a new challenge is a part of what makes us motivated and compelled to engage.

Meaningful Choices

Langer's research with older adults who live in nursing homes, many of whom people believe can no longer improve their memories, can teach us about student motivation. Her team found that offering small choices to nursing home residents resulted in longer lives (Langer & Rodin, 1976), which in part is interpreted as the desire to engage in life longer. In another study, they offered rewards to nursing home residents to remember things like the nurses' names. Over time the difficulty increased with what the residents were asked to memorize. Researchers found that the residents' memories improved with these novel and challenging tasks, even for patients who medical professionals believed there was little chance of improvement.

It is not just novelty and productive struggle that is motivating but also having choices. Research with students using the self-determination theory of motivation (Ryan & Deci, 2000) shows that choice can be motivating when the options meet the students' need for autonomy, competence, and relatedness. Choice is motivating when the options are relevant to the students' interests and goals. The options cannot be too numerous or complex. Additionally, the options need to be aligned with the students' values and culture (Katz & Assor, 2006). When we offer students choices, make sure they have novelty, and adequate amounts of challenge, as they are more likely to feel motivated and a desire to engage. Not all choices are motivating, so considering your students and the particular options you want to make available are key.

When offering students choices, consider the following:

- Are the options relevant to students?
- Are there enough options but not too many?
- Are there options that every student can access?
- Do the options match students' values and cultures?
- Do the choices have novelty built in?

Productive Struggle

We can also look at motivation through the lens of joy. When we experience joy in our bodies, it is because of the release of dopamine and serotonin, two types of neurotransmitters in the brain (Lahoti, 2023). These chemicals feel good in the moment and teach our bodies to seek more of them. This is a natural way our bodies help us stay motivated to experience the pleasure of learning (Rock, 2014). Our circulatory systems are also involved in the feelings of joy. We tend to get flushed, feel butterflies in our stomach, and to physically change our posture, all of which are initiated by the circulatory system. Going back to Chapter 3, the autonomic nervous system is also involved in feeling joy. Our pupils dilate, our heart rate speeds up, and our saliva increases. These physiological experiences of joy happen in part because students are able to work through a challenge and then get the physical rewards of it feeling good. I tend to call this the learner's high, and it is not that different from the high a runner gets after finishing a race. Motivation is not just thoughts in our mind but also physiological responses to working through something challenging.

The research on working through something challenging is often referred to as productive struggle. In one study of productive struggle, eight-year-olds were divided into two groups. One group practiced throwing bean bags at a target from three feet away.

The other group practiced throwing the bean bags at a target from two and four feet away, varying the practice distance. After twelve weeks the two groups were asked to throw the beanbag to hit a target that was three feet away. The group that had the varied practice outperformed the group who only practiced from three feet away consistently (Kerr & Booth, 1978). One conclusion drawn from this study is that varied practice and productive struggle create stronger brain pathways called myelin (Sriram, 2020). Myelin makes brain signals faster and stronger.

> A well-myelinated brain signal travels over 100 times faster than an unmyelinated brain signal. When students first learn a skill, the connections between neurons are weak—much like a dirt path. Mastery occurs when those neural connections are constructed into freeways by the accumulation of myelin. So how do you help students go from dirt paths to freeways? By creating desirable difficulty through productive struggle. (Sriram, 2020, paras. 7–8)

This means that creating context for productive struggle helps motivate students by bringing in elements of novelty and challenge, as well as helping to promote learning through the creation of myelin in the brain. The following table shows ways to bring more productive struggle into learning experiences.

Ways to Bring More Productive Struggle Into Learning Experiences

Type	Examples
Variation	• Types of reading experience (independent read, partner read, read-aloud, etc.) • Types of texts (short story, article, poem, novel, podcast, video, etc.) • Types of writing experiences (about a text, about life, about an issue, etc.)
Time	• Quick reads and writes • Longer, multi-period read and writes
Amount of Teacher Support	• Where you begin in the gradual release of responsibility model (I go, we go, you go) • Preview a text or not for students
Integration	• Integrate texts from across days/weeks/units • Integrate ideas from across time and texts • Integrate strategies from across lessons/units

HOW DOES MINDFULNESS HELP STUDENTS?

At this point we all know the term *mindfulness* and it can lead you to either roll your eyes or lean in with glee depending on your prior experiences. In this book I draw on mindfulness as a scientific concept that is defined by the American Psychological Association (n.d.) as "awareness of one's internal states and surroundings." Awareness is tied to one's ability to "notice differences" and nuance (Langer, 2024, p. 205). The ability to notice differences without judgment is a key factor in collaboration and engagement. Without awareness our students cannot directly pay attention.

Increase in Engagement

In one study, autistic children interacted with adults by playing games. The researchers video recorded and noticed how degrees of adult mindfulness impacted the children. The adults were instructed to be more or less mindful depending on the group they were put in. For example, the less mindful adults were told to be positive when playing the games but to only pretend to be interested in what the child was doing. The adults in the highly mindful group were told to be positive as well but were also told to "focus on the variability of the child's behavior and the emergence of novel elements in their emotional expression" (Langer, 2024, p. 193). They were directed to notice the child's body language, voice, inflection, and general state of being. This paying attention and noticing was framed as studying the child to "understand their internal state."

After analyzing the video recordings, the researchers found that the children who interacted with more mindful adults showed greater fun behaviors and showed fewer avoidance behaviors. They also showed an increase in collaborative behaviors and engaged interaction. This led to the conclusion that when the adults were more mindful, they helped the children become more engaged. The focused awareness and nuanced noticing also led the adults to get to know the children better. Basically, both child and adult showed more engagement and were better able to read one another.

In another study, researchers studied patients suffering from traumatic brain injury and the relatives who were their caregivers. They found a correlation between the mindfulness of the caregiver and the functioning of the patient. They concluded "mindful caregivers are likely to attend to the variability in symptoms and responses for those for whom they are caring" (Langer, 2024, p. 195). The ability to remain curious (another way of being mindful) had a huge impact on the people they cared for and on themselves.

"When caregivers start to notice small changes in the symptoms of the people for whom they are caring, several things happen. They become more mindful themselves, which is . . . good for their own health. And when caregivers are more engaged and optimistic, their jobs seem a bit easier and burnout becomes less likely" (Langer, 2024, p. 195). Langer goes on to explain that moving from global thinking (everything, always) to more specific thinking (sometimes) helps people feel better, develop awareness, and be more present. In a profession like teaching, where we often feel we have little control over many variables, it can be helpful to realize that this one shift, bringing a lens of mindful curiosity and specificity, can help us and our students feel more engaged.

A LOOK IN THE MIRROR

Consider the following research findings about curiosity:

- The stronger the desire to find out, the greater the activation in the reward network (Kang et al., 2009).
- The brain's reward networks activate in response to things that bring joy and deactivate in response to things that reduce enjoyment (Waytz & Mason, 2014).

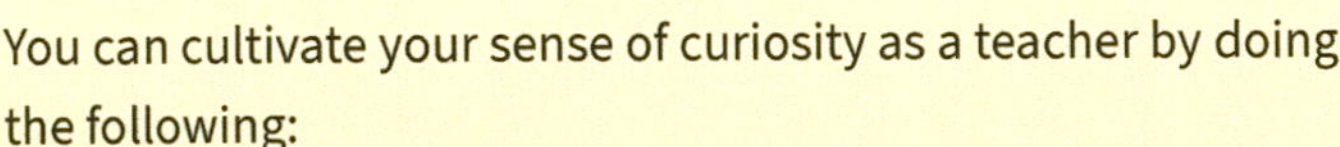

You can cultivate your sense of curiosity as a teacher by doing the following:

- Turning judgments or opinions about students into questions.
    - Example: My opinion is that students tune out when their classmates share because they are egocentric. Turned into a question: Why do students seem to tune each other out? When do they tune out? When do they tune in? What seems to pique students' attention?
- Teaching a different text or topic.
    - Simply working within a new text or topic that you don't already know well can lead you to be more curious and pay more attention to the specific details.
    - Example: I usually teach this short story, but I could use this podcast or this story instead.
- Noticing nuance.
    - Example: Instead of using the words *always* and *never*, find some students to focus on and spend time noticing the nuances of when and how. Instead of thinking this student "never reads," consider when do they, for how long, and in what kinds of texts.
    - Use the nuanced noticings to look at your own teaching too. Instead of thinking I am not a good teacher of ____, think about when and where you feel confident, what the context is, and what happens before, during, and after those moments. Study yourself with nuance as well.

Your degree of mindfulness has a significant impact on the motivation of others. In one study, magazine sales people were divided into two groups. One group was instructed to treat every potential customer exactly the same with the same sales pitch. The second group was instructed to be mindful of the potential customer and to vary their pitch in new and subtle ways for each person. As I read this study I could not help but think about how some districts are handing teachers scripts and telling them to teach all of their students in the same (mindless) way. But, back to this study. The customers who received the mindful sales pitch later described the sales person as more charismatic and they were more likely to purchase the magazines from the mindful pitches (Langer, 2024, p. 184). This finding led the researchers to the conclusion that mindfulness can shape the behaviors of other people around the mindful person.

Self-Esteem and a Positive Perspective

Another study based on the idea that mindfulness impacted the others around the person took place at a boy's summer camp. The boys in the study were assigned a researcher to interview them and the researchers posed as coaches. One set of "coaches" were instructed to be mindful and notice changes in the child's verbal and nonverbal behavior across the interview. The other coaches were told to be mindless and just pretend to be interested in the boys. Both coach groups were told to be positive. After the interviews the boys were given a test of their self-esteem and asked about their overall camp experience. The researchers had already accounted for prior levels of the boy's self-esteem before selecting the participants and putting them into groups. "The children who interacted with a mindless adult had significantly lower self-esteem scores and an expressed dislike of both the camp and the interviewer than campers interacting with a mindful adult" (Langer, 2024, p. 186).

The study has connections to us educators. Our degree of mindfulness, our ability to pay attention and notice differences in our students, has a huge impact on their self-esteem and their view of reading in general. When we are more mindful of our students, they will tend to feel better about themselves as learners and look more positively on the act of reading. Both teachers and students benefit from nuanced and intentional noticing (mindfulness).

Attention to Detail

Let's look at one more study (of many more possible studies) on the impact of a mindful person in a learning environment. Researchers wrote the words from *Mary Had a Little Lamb* on an index card and included an error by adding a second "a." The card read "Mary had a a little lamb." Participants came into a room and sat down next to another person and were asked to read the card. Most readers did not notice the error and when asked to count the number of words on the card said five words even though there were six. The participants who were seated next to a person who was instructed to be mindful were much more likely to notice the error. This happened even though the person who was mindfully sitting did not interact with the reader, nor did the reader know anything about the mindful neighbor. This study was conducted another time, but the mindful person sitting next to the reader had just finished meditating in a different room before coming in to sit down. In this case all of the readers who were seated next to a recent meditator read the sentence correctly and noticed the error (Langer, 2024, p. 187).

As teachers, we have likely all felt frustrated when students don't seem to be paying close enough attention as they read, write, and complete their work. What if the ways to support them included our own ability to be more mindful and to make the practice of noticing nuanced differences a key part of our days? Many of the skills we teach are actually tied to being mindful. Take a look at the chart that follows. In this chart you'll see how mindfulness and the ability to notice differences is a key reading comprehension skill across contexts as well as part of self-monitoring and self-awareness. Use this chart as a guide for lessons that teach students explicitly how to be mindful. You can work your way down this chart by teaching a lesson on each mindful practice. For example, model how you notice what you do as you read a picture book, short story, article, or video. Use the language on this chart as you model. Then give students a few minutes to try it out themselves as they read.

MINDFUL READERS CHART (APPENDIX N)

Notice what they do as they read.	"First I . . . then I . . ."
Notice their thinking as they read	"I'm wondering about . . ."
Notice their feelings as they read.	"I am feeling . . ."
Notice changes.	"This changed when . . ."
Notice differences between characters/topics.	"These are different because . . ."
Notice differences between perspectives.	"I see it like this . . ., and my partner sees it like . . ."

A LOOK IN THE MIRROR

All of the moves mindful students make apply to us teachers. We can use the same ways of being as teachers to be more mindful of what students are doing.

MINDFUL TEACHERS

Notice what students do as they read.	"First you . . ., then you . . ."
Notice student thinking as they read.	"You are wondering about . . ."
Notice student feelings as they read.	"You are feeling . . ."
Notice changes.	"This changed for you when . . ."
Notice differences between characters/topics.	"You see these are different because . . ."
Notice differences between perspectives.	"You see it like this . . ., and your partner sees it like . . ."

One concrete way to be a more mindful teacher is to avoid generalizations about students such as they are right or they are good at inferring. These are really labels that don't allow us to slow down, notice, and see variance—the hallmarks of mindfulness and effective teaching. Practice your ability to notice and name what students are doing. I find it easier to first notice and name nuance in written work because I can look back at it several times. Then I practice noticing and naming when listening to students talk, which tends to be harder for me because it moves so fast and I only get one listen.

Take a few minutes to be mindful. Jot down what you notice about yourself and your students. Creating a regular routine of writing down our mindful noticings allows us to recognize patterns.

Let's practice being mindful together as we look at this transcript of a student conversation halfway through their reading of the book *Pizza and Taco: Too Cool for School,* by Stephen Shaskan.

- What do you notice?
- Can you name at least three things you learned about each student?
- Can you see any small, nuanced difference between the two students?

Ava: Pizza is really trying to be cool. I think he is embarrassed by Taco.

Eamon: Totally. Taco is so cringe.

Ava and Eamon laugh.

Eamon: He is trying too hard to be cool. That makes him [interrupted by Ava]

Ava: uncool.

Eamon: Yes!

Eamon: But even though the characters are food and not kids, they seem kind of young, like maybe second graders. Maybe even first graders.

Ava: Really? I didn't think so. I thought they were more like our age.

When discussing this transcript with teachers we noticed the following about these students: they

- identified the main characters to focus on (Pizza and Taco),
- thought about the character motivation (wanted to seem cool),
- inferred the potential conflict (trying too hard to be cool),
- inferred the character's age/grade,
- listened to one another and agreed ("totally" and "yes"),
- disagreed respectfully ("I thought they were more our age"),
- interrupted to add on ("uncool"),
- took an intellectual risk (using the word *maybe*), and
- connected with each other (laughed together).

This sort of mindful attention helps us get to know the students better, reinforce strengths, and decide on targeted next steps. As their teacher I could choose any of the items on this list to give them positive feedback on. Then I could look at my unit plans or standards to decide what to teach them next. For example, maybe I would show them how to use their ideas to make predictions or notice when the characters shift and think about why.

HOW CAN WE MAKE READING FUN IN ANY DISCIPLINE?

We might assume that if students are focused, able to handle challenges, and motivated to learn, they will also be having fun. This may be the case, but we can take a deeper look at what we mean by fun and design learning experiences that are more intentionally fun producing for students.

First, let's look at what fun is not. We may think that fun is prizes, games, and easy-peasy silly activities. For example, we may think it is fun to color in a picture of a favorite character from a book we read. Some may think it is fun to play Kahoot! and compete to win a game that asks you to answer questions about a topic. Others may think that it is fun to talk to friends and make book recommendations. The thing is, fun is not actually the same for everyone and fun is not inherent in the activity itself, but it does include the qualities the activity provides. Let's take a deeper dive.

For a student who loves to make art, enjoys the challenge of coloring within the lines, and then gets to share that art with others, they may find character coloring pages fun. For someone else, they may feel stressed and lack confidence in their ability to color within the lines. They may take too long to really color well and then feel rushed and anxious about the same activity. Fun is not static; rather, it is contextual and personal.

Price (2021), author of the book *The Power of Fun*, calls "true fun" the kind of fun where energy rushes "through her like a spark" (p. 13). Price goes on to explain that true fun "is the feeling of being fully present and engaged, free from self-criticism and judgment" (p. 13). She further describes three main elements that create true fun. First, we are in a state of flow and are fully present in what we are doing. Second, we bring a playfulness into the experience. Third, true fun helps us feel a sense of connection to others. In other words, "true fun is the confluence of playfulness, connection, and flow" (p. 32).

Playful Readers

The word *playfulness* can make us think of silly and frivolous time, something we may be able to squeeze in on the days before a holiday break or on a Friday afternoon. But Price (2021) defines playfulness as "a feeling of lightheartedness and freedom" (p. 32). Think about the moments of getting so lost in a book that you lose your own sense of reality and are transported into the scene yourself. Playfulness is also apparent when a class is engrossed in a class read-aloud and then bursts into discussions when asked to react to what just happened. Readers can also experience playfulness when they debate a peer and play devil's advocate, enjoying the competitive nature of proving a point. If done in a lighthearted way, engaged reading and reacting often feels playful. I tend to think of playfulness as a no-risk or low-risk experience where students can lean into the text without worrying about how others will judge them.

Psychologists distinguish work from play by the type of reward the experience produces. If the activity is done for an extrinsic reward (grades, praise, etc.), it is being viewed as work. On the other hand, if the experience is done for an intrinsic reward (joy, connection, self-confidence, interest, etc.), it is viewed as play (Pink, 2009). So, reading, writing, and engaging in discussions are not in and of themselves playful, but they can absolutely be viewed as play if intrinsic value is experienced.

SOME WAYS TO FRAME READING AS PLAY

- Remove the stakes: aim for low- or no-stakes practice.
- Let go of (or minimize) external measures and judgments.
- Offer choice (see pages 86–87).
- Build time in for self-reflection and celebration.
- Establish time for checking in with how you feel as you read and normalize laughing and smiling.
- Read aloud rich texts (to students of all ages).
- Carve out frequent opportunities to react, respond, and share with one another.
- Check that not all books you read are tearjerkers or archaic primary sources, and vary the genres and tone.

For those of you who work in schools with scripted curriculum, you can still modify the lessons to consider some of the elements of play. For example, add in a high-interest read-aloud to get students engaged before asking them to read something more dry on their own. In between scripted lessons, build in reflection time and time to talk with peers about their experiences.

Reading Connections

Price (2021) defines connection as "the feeling of having a special, shared experience with someone (or something)" (p. 33). This does not necessarily mean asking students to make superficial connections to the books they are reading such as "Have you ever ______ like this character?" It means you feel a part of a community and through that community you can be yourself. I wrote a book called *Teach Like Yourself* (Goldberg, 2018) because of the need for teachers and students to be able to be their authentic selves in the classroom. This is essential for many reasons, including the way it helps us experience an activity as true fun. Research and experience show that when we are authentic, our students are more likely to connect with us and want to be their most authentic selves too.

When we are connected to the texts we read, we care about the characters or topics, we get lost in the world of the text, and we somehow identify with the themes. During a recent student-led conversation in an eleventh-grade English class of mostly boys, the students shared that they think the best books are ones where the themes are both relatable and get them to think about their own lives. In their own ways, they went on to discuss how connection is essential to them as readers. They even discussed how a book that was super challenging for them at first became less challenging because of the connections they felt to the themes.

Bishop's (1990) work on books as windows, mirrors, and sliding glass doors also highlights the importance of connection. When students read books that are mirrors to their own lives, they are sent the message that their lives matter, that they are not alone, and that someone else has been through the same things they are experiencing. These sorts of connections are essential for all students and are one of the reasons why schools are closely auditing the books in their libraries to ensure more books match the lived experiences of their students. Everyone needs to have opportunities to read books that mirror their lives and offer connections for many reasons, including the likelihood that they may experience more fun while reading.

Ways to Foster Reading Connections

Texts	• Provide a variety of texts that are mirrors for every student in the class. • Develop text sets in which there are multiple texts by the same author, about a similar setting, or tackle a similar theme.
Talk	• Pair up students with similar interests or identities to talk about their connections to a text. • Create frequent opportunities for students to make connections with one another around texts. Think book talks, book recommendations, and book clubs.
Topics	• Provide choice so students can read about topics they feel connected to. • Develop multimodal text sets that include video, audio, visual, and print texts all focused on the same topic (see page 22 for an example).

One way to encourage more text connections is to start a chart with students like the one that follows. Older students can also create good reads accounts that offer many text connection ideas like this one, crowdsourced by other readers.

If you liked . . .	You may like . . .
Amulet series	Zita series *Little Robot* City of Ember series
Chasing Lincoln's Killer	*An Officer and a Spy* *Spies: The Secret Showdown Between America and Russia* *Freewater*

Reading Flow

Mihaly Csikszentmihalyi coined the term *flow* to describe the experiences people described with the metaphor of "being carried by a current like a river flows." In his studies, the participants experienced flow "when the activity was difficult and involved risk. It usually stretched the person's capacity and provided a challenge" (Biasutti, 2011). Price (2021) describes flow as being so engrossed in the current experience that you lose track of time.

Anyone who identifies as a reader, no matter their age or subject areas, has experienced reading flow. I recall this experience vividly as a young child reading the book *Bridge to Terabithia,* by Katherine Paterson. I sobbed into my Mickey and Minnie comforter on the couch; my mom ran into the room to see if I was OK. I was shocked back into the reality of the room where I was sitting when she asked, "Are you OK?" At that moment I was taken out of reading flow and had to recalibrate back into my own body. During bedtime stories, young children often ask us to read "just one more page" not just to delay going to sleep but also because they are so engaged in the story. Even teens have shared the ways they stayed up way too late having to finish a book because there was no way they could sleep without finding out what happened.

Reading flow can sometimes be supported best by thinking about what gets in the way of it. The following table lists some very common practices that, while well intentioned, often interrupt or prevent reading flow from happening. If given the time and space to focus on reading, most students will experience flow. The key is to implement many of the tenets from this entire section so they can stay focused, feel motivated, handle difficulty, and have fun. If any of the following practices are still up and running in your classroom, consider alternatives that may accomplish your goals without interrupting flow.

Common Practices That May Prevent Reading Flow and What to Try Instead

Instead of	Try This
Assigning questions to answer after every chapter or section	Work with students to develop a few essential questions to pursue across the whole text. Teach students how to carry a conversation across days and across a text around those questions.
Requiring a certain number of annotations per page or section	Model what is worth annotating and why. Focus on how the annotations help students understand. Reflect together and make a chart of what we focus on as we annotate and how it helps us.
Segmenting a book into small chunks and slowly taking the entire class through the book over several weeks	Mentor students in mapping out a text into meaning parts so they read the text in no more than a few weeks. Show them how to make a reading plan on a calendar for how many pages they hope to read each day. During the first few days ask students to reflect on how it's going and adjust their plan as needed.
Assigning specific types of journal responses	Show students the value of documenting their thinking in meaningful ways. Focus on how writing about reading helps us find patterns in our thinking and deepen our thinking. Tie this to the essential questions across a text so students can focus on depth.
Holding students back from reading ahead	If students are really invested in what happens next and the pace of the class is slowing them down, consider picking up the pace, grouping students based on their pacing so they can discuss with others who read faster, or add in other choice-based texts that can keep them reading.

Round robin reading	Research shows this can have a negative impact on comprehension and cause anxiety. Instead, choose to read aloud, choral read (in primary grades), or independently read and then discuss.
Offering only a few minutes per day to read in class	Larger chunks of time, on fewer days if needed. Help students get lost in the text and build some momentum. Try for at least fifteen minutes a few days a week.
Assigning all reading for homework	Carve out time in class for reading. Once students get engaged in the text, then some of it can be done at home. Make sure they can actually read the text independently if it is homework.
Breaking up reading with other assignments that require them to shift back and forth between reading and writing frequently	No one has enough time, so it makes sense to shift back and forth between reading and writing, but it can interrupt flow. Try to focus for at least a few days or weeks on one as the major element while the other is the minor element and then switch.

A SUMMARY OF KEY IDEAS FROM CHAPTER 4

This section took a deep dive into how body and brain integration helps students handle difficulty, get motivated, and experience reading across content areas as more fun.

- Stamina is dependent on how long we expect the experience to last. Remember the two-thirds rule when helping students avoid fatigue and avoid losing focus.
- Students' perception of difficulty can be minimized by having a trusted person nearby. Having a peer or teacher be a supportive presence makes challenges feel less daunting.
- When we change the sequence of experiences, we can often handle more challenges with ease.
- Students are motivated by having intentional choices and by experiencing the right amount of varied, productive struggle.
- When students are in proximity to a teacher who is mindful, they are often able to pay more attention, build self-confidence, and notice more nuance. There are also payoffs for mindful teachers, such as avoiding burnout and feeling more successful by noticing small amounts of growth.
- Students experience reading as fun when they are playful, connected, and in flow. We can design classroom experiences that help students have more opportunities to feel the intrinsic rewards of reading.

A SUMMARY OF PRACTICES FROM CHAPTER 4

Practice	Reflection Questions	When and Where I May Use This
Consider stamina and the two-thirds rule when planning for the whole period (page 76).	How can I use the two-thirds rule and help students focus for longer periods of time? Are there clocks and timers I may want to stop using with students?	
Teach students why and how to be a supportive partner (page 80).	Are there new pairings I might want to try? How might I be more explicit in my teaching about how to be a supportive partner?	
Consider changing the sequence in lessons (page 85).	Which units or lesson sequences do I want to try this with? Where can I group texts in a way so I start with more complexity?	
Offer meaningful choices (page 86).	How can I get feedback from students about the sort of choices they are currently getting? Want to have?	
Plan for and teach students why they need productive struggle (page 87).	What is my relationship to struggle? How can I get more comfortable with productive struggle? How am I framing productive struggles for students? Do they understand the benefits?	

(Continued)

(Continued)

Teach students what it means to be a mindful reader. Model each quality they need to learn (page 94).	How might I use this chart for formative assessment of students? How can I model more mindful reading for students in whole group or small group lessons?	
Reflect on your own teacher mindful noticing (page 95).	How will I practice more mindful noticing? Which colleagues do I want to reach out to so we can practice this together?	
Reflect on how you frame reading. Intentionally frame it as play (page 100).	How do students view reading? As work or play? How is my language framing reading?	
Foster different kinds of reading connections (page 101).	Where do I feel connected to my curriculum? Where do the students feel connected? How can I let go of parts where students disconnect to make room for more peer and text connections?	
Replace practices that get in the way of reading flow (page 104).	What does reading flow feel like in my body? How do students feel reading flow in their bodies? Which practices can I try to create more space for reading flow?	

Chapter 5

Students Learn Through Movement

"Our thoughts—even, or especially, those of an abstract or symbolic nature—are powerfully shaped by the way we move our bodies."

— Paul (2021, p. 53)

PRIME YOURSELF

As you begin this section bring your attention to what and how you visualize as you read this excerpt from *Clap When You Land* by Elizabeth Acevedo.

> He is technically the entire neighborhood's pet,
> a dog with no name but the title of stray;
> ever since he was a pup he's slept outside our door
> & even if I don't think of him as solely mine,
> I know he thinks of me as his.
> I throw him the heel of bread from the loaf

- What did you picture as you read?
- Are the pictures in your mind still, or do they have movement?
- What perspective did you take on? That of the narrator? The dog? An observer?
- If you were to talk to someone about what you just read, how might you move your hands to describe the events? Characters? Setting?

As you read the word *throw*, it activated the same part of your brain (your motor system) as if you did throw the bread. And your choice to picture the dog from afar or picture yourself as the dog was impacted by how you feel about dogs. You'll learn a whole lot more about these concepts and more in this chapter. The more we become aware of how we read and understand, the more we can better understand and teach our students to do the same. In this chapter, we'll closely look at how our motor systems and movements impact our understanding and our teaching.

For more than a decade, teachers, mostly of younger grades, have incorporated movement breaks into their classrooms. This is often due to students getting fidgety and the availability of free internet resources that lead students through short dancing, yoga, and breathing exercises. Often though, the movement is seen as a break from the learning, not the vehicle for the actual learning itself.

Young children spend about fifty percent of their days sitting in chairs, and that amount increases as they move up through the grades (Paul, 2021). This is based on the outdated yet prevalent idea that "while we're thinking, we believe, we should be sitting still" (p. 46). Numerous studies across disciplines have shown that movement increases all of the following:

- Attention
- Engagement
- Confidence
- Empathy
- Productivity
- Executive function
- Abstract thinking
- Memory
- Comprehension
- Communication
- Conceptual understanding

This section focuses on the research and practical applications for incorporating purposeful movement into lessons as a vehicle for learning. Some of the ideas will confirm what you have likely intuitively understood and witnessed as a teacher, and some of the ideas challenge our taken-for-granted "truths." I trust you will read with an open mind and then bring curiosity to trying some of the practices out with your students.

You will learn about

- movement's key role in memory,
- ways reading skills across content areas are impacted by the motor system, and
- five types of movement and how they support learning.

HOW IS MEMORY ENHANCED THROUGH MOVEMENT?

Notice how often you find your body creating a movement—a sway, dip, gesture, or facial expression—as a way to tap into a past memory. It happens so often we likely don't even recognize it is happening. As a former child gymnast, I can still remember every twist, turn, jump, and flip of my routines, even though it has been over thirty years since I performed them. My body remembers, not just because of the repetition but also because of the physicality and the ways my mind and body worked together with intention. The same sort of dynamic is helpful when understanding how students can enhance their memory for what they are reading and learning about.

Science writer Paul (2021) describes the benefits of movement on memory in her book *The Extended Mind: The Power of Thinking Outside the Brain.* "Linking movement to the material to be recalled creates a richer and therefore more indelible memory trace in the brain" (p. 54). Let's step back and look at a few different kinds of memory and how they are connected to movement.

Procedural memory is focused on how to do something. This might mean remembering how to wash your hands, how to ride a bike, and how to write a complete sentence. There are many procedures that students learn that directly and indirectly relate to being a student. Likely the first week of school (or longer) is dedicated to the teaching of routines with the hope that it will lead to procedural memory. It can be helpful to make a list of these procedures and to ask yourself, "How could movement be incorporated into these routines?" The following chart shows a few examples that can inspire you to create your own movements connected to procedures.

Movement and Procedural Memory Examples

Classroom Procedures	Movement Examples
Gathering at a whole class meeting area for teaching	Gesturing up with your hands and then pointing to the meeting area
Getting out and organizing materials	Coming up with an acronym for what students need and using movement to go along with it can be helpful for memory. For example, you might come up with the 3T's. "Get out your text, tools, and tablet" could be associated with you putting up a finger for each T like a list.
Reading a chart on the wall to prepare for class	Pointing to the chart and then your head as you say, "Please read this chart and think about our goal for the day."
Coming back together as a class after small group or partner conversations	Pointing to your eyes as you say, "Eyes on me," or making a circle with your hands to show it is time to circle back up as a class.

Declarative memory is focused on the information about a topic or event. This might mean remembering the details of a lecture, the facts about an animal's habitat, or the events leading up to a battle. Declarative memory is used anytime you ask a student to remember what something is or means, such as the definition of an idiom or the details about the setting in a story you just read.

When movement is connected to the information we are learning, it creates what is called an *enactment effect.* The enactment effect calls on us to use both procedural

and declarative memory in tandem, and as a result our ability to recall is stronger. If you are an early childhood educator, think about how adding movement to letter identification and phoneme segmentation increases students' ability to remember letters and sounds. If you are a teacher of older students, think about how role playing and acting out a scene helps students remember key details. Creating the context for the enactment effect can boost students' memories in both learning procedures and recalling information.

One study of actors conducted by Noice et al. (2000) found that actors remember the lines from plays they performed with ninety percent accuracy even months after the play ended and after they had already taken on new roles. They found this happened in conjunction with the blocking, which is the planning out of the physical movements on stage that coincide with the dialogue. It was the physical movements of the actors' bodies and their gestures that helped them remember the lines.

After the findings of this study with actors, the researchers went on to use similar acting techniques that incorporated movement and dialogue memorization with non-actors aged sixty-five to eighty-five. After a four-week program that used rehearsal and performance of a scene, the participants scored higher in overall cognitive performance such as word memory, verbal fluency, and problem solving (Noice et al., 2000. The researchers found that the participants were able to apply what they learned about how to link movement to information being learned to other aspects of their lives to boost their memory in general.

Additional studies of movement and memory were conducted with undergraduate students (Noice & Noice, 2001). These researchers found that students who incorporated movement into their learning remembered seventy-six percent of the material while those who didn't incorporate movement but used more traditional memorization strategies recalled only thirty-seven percent. These studies revealed the pattern that "information that has become associated with a movement is better remembered when we reproduce that same movement later when we are calling it up from memory" (Paul, 2021, p. 56).

The research conducted by Noice and Noice (2001, 2007) found that even if the movement could not be performed, such as during a final exam, it was still beneficial for memory. This is because the intention to move in connection with information creates a sort of tag that acts as a mental marker that it is important. When students can identify what is important to remember and then add a movement to it, there is a higher likelihood that they will be able to recall it. Our job as teachers is to both help them determine what is important enough to put to memory and to learn ways to incorporate movement into the learning of the material. Noice and Noice (2007) claim, "[O]ne might paraphrase Descartes and say I move, therefore I remember" (p. 2).

Ways to Incorporate Movement and Create Memory Tags

When we want to remember . . .	Look for . . .	Try out . . .	Photo Examples
Plot points for retelling	Character actions (verbs)	Making the actions the character makes with our own bodies	
Main ideas in informational text	Bold words, headings, and repeated ideas	Acting out the information (e.g., Make your body fly like a bird) Say the main idea while also creating a gesture to go with it (e.g., Draw a box in the air)	
Details that support ideas	Examples, non-examples, lists, and visuals	Using your fingers to connect ideas (e.g., Touch the top of the finger to state the big idea and then move down your finger as you state the details)	
Comparisons	Similarities and differences	Making a Venn diagram with your gestures (e.g., Each hand is a different item being compared, so raise that hand while you say the information and put your hands together when the information is the same for both)	

A LOOK IN THE MIRROR

It is not just students, but also us educators, who could also use a boost in our memory. We can also use the power of enactment effect to help us recall lesson ideas, information about our students, and text details.

Pause and note which information you want to remember from this chapter so far. Jot it down. Now add some movement to it. Here are a few ideas.

- To remember what procedural memory is, you might use your fingers to count 1, 2, 3 as you place a finger in the air. This could tag the information as something to remember and also remind you that it has to do with sequence and steps.
- To remember what declarative memory is, you might point to an imaginary list of facts in the air or draw a web in the air. These movements could help you connect the term to the concept of remembering information about a topic.
- To remember to try out more movement connected to information in your classroom, create your own action. What will help you connect your intention to try it out with the concept itself?

HOW ARE READING SKILLS CONNECTED TO BODY MOVEMENTS?

Some of the reading skills that we were taught were solely brain based are connected to physical movement. This includes movement in our own body and also by watching others move their bodies. We can learn from perceiving others' movements and then replaying those movements in our own nervous systems. As a teacher, you've likely noticed that students end up mirroring your body language and hand movements, not to mock you but as clues that they are taking in your physical movement as well as your words. Let's look at how two key reading skills are connected to movement.

- Envisioning is impacted by grammar and the ways we mentally simulate movement.
- Inferences happen when we experience cognitive empathy while watching someone else's experience and feeling it in our own bodies.

Envisioning

Studies show that grammar impacts the envisioning or mental simulation the student experiences when trying to comprehend a text. The student will either take on a participant perspective or an observer perspective. This impacts not just the understanding but also the movement and mental simulation the student is doing (Bergen, 2012).

Bergen (2012) illustrates the ways grammar impacts our understanding of a sentence. For example, in this sentence, "*The driver gripped the steering wheel and pounded on the horn as he waited for the light to change,*" the writer chose third person. Because this is written in third person, most people will mentally simulate this sentence from an observer perspective. They will be watching the driver's movements from behind or above. If the sentence is written with second person language, "*You gripped the steering wheel and pounded on the horn as you waited for the light to change,*" it is more likely that the reader will take on a participant perspective. This means you are in the seat seeing the actions you are doing.

Studies show that the perspective you take on is not random but influenced by your own attitudes. People are more likely to take on a participant perspective when they have a positive attitude toward the events. When a text is written in first person and the reader is unclear who the "I" is referring to, they are more likely to take on a participant perspective and see themselves performing the actions (Bergen, 2012).

Implications for teaching are to be aware of the grammar in the text that students are reading and notice the perspective they are taking on when they mentally simulate the actions. You can figure this out by asking them to sketch or describe what they are seeing in their mind's eye. You can also notice the pronouns they use when retelling what they read. Are they talking about the characters in first person? If so, you have a big clue they are reading and mentally simulating the text from a participant perspective. Rather than correct this as a mistake, you can coach the student to keep visualizing from this perspective as it helps them with understanding and to also use the character's names when talking about it to others to avoid confusion.

This ability to take on a participant perspective is essential when developing empathy. We also know that students today are experiencing less empathy than previous generations (Turkle, 2015) and that many businesses claim that empathy is the most important leadership skill (Brower, 2021). We can intentionally model how we take on a participant perspective and then create some shared experiences for students to do the same.

Envisioning Lesson Example

In one lesson I projected a few pages from a graphic novel, *Little Robot* by Ben Hatke, and students pretended to be the characters. They acted out the character's movements and then generated verbs and adverbs to go along with the image. My job was to coach them and scribe what they said. Students worked in pairs and then shared with the whole class.

This was the image I projected from pages 26–27 of Little Robot.

Students generated verbs and adverbs after taking on a participant perspective. I jotted down their words on a chart. I asked them to act like the character, name the action word (verb), and describe how they did it (adverb). The following chart was created as a class from the list of words they shared.

Verbs	Adverbs
• struggle • wrestle • wriggle • attempt • practice	• quickly • cautiously • slowly • carefully • repeatedly

Several of the students who participated in this lesson have a diagnosis of neurodivergence and perspective taking is not considered one of their strengths. It took almost fifteen minutes of modeling and coaching for students to really understand the process. We did not give up and repeated the process of acting and naming several times. Eventually, all students participated and contributed.

Teachers and I noticed that by acting out the actions together, these students began to take on the participant perspective more and speak with more empathy about the characters. If you have students who are similar, this sort of lesson can be helpful. This lesson was not only fun and engaging, but it also incorporated intentional movement to aid in comprehension, reinforced student's declarative memory of what verbs and adverbs are, and developed their vocabulary. You can do this with any image across content areas.

Inference and Social Imagination

While there are many different kinds of inferences, gap-filling and social inferences (keys to empathy) are two types that are clearly tied to our body-brain experience. Our bodies help us develop empathy because seeing and feeling are connected (Niedenthal, 2007). Research has shown that "we understand others by replaying their behavior in our own motor system as if we are performing the behavior ourselves" (S. Beilock, 2015). This motor system connection helps us understand that inference is an embodied skill.

Professor and educator Peter Johnston explains the importance of social imagination as a life skill and reading skill in his seminal work, *Choice Words.* Social imagination entails being able to infer "what others are feeling, to read people's faces and expressions, to imagine different perspectives, to make sense of abstract ideas, and to reason through this" (Keier, 2012, para. 3). The skill of social imagination is often couched in reading questions such as "Why did the character make that choice?" and "How does the character feel?" and "What does the characterization reveal about the person?" Our bodies help us with the ability to develop the cognitive empathy needed to answer these sorts of questions. For example, embodied research found that making facial expressions helps you understand what the other person or character is feeling (Niedenthal et al., 2010). A simple three-step process can help support social imagination inferences.

THREE-STEP PROCESS FOR USING MOVEMENT TO SUPPORT SOCIAL IMAGINATION INFERENCES

1. Look at the person's facial expression, or read the description of the character's body language.
2. Make *your* facial expression match what you saw, or make *your* body language match what you read.
3. Ask yourself, "What feeling am I having now?" while performing the facial or body posture.

Let's look at an example. In the picture book *John's Turn*, by Mac Barnett, we can make some inferences about John's feelings and motivations as he stands on stage, in front of his peers, about to dance alone. In the text it says,

> Mr. Ross pressed play.
>
> The music was strings, violins and things, and then maybe flutes.

A bunch of kids laughed.

Mr. K shushed the crowd.

Then it was John's turn.

The illustrations that correspond to the page show John's face and body posture. Students can take a moment to zoom in on John's face and make that face themselves and feel in their own bodies what sensations are associated with that face. They may be feeling a drop in their stomach and some tension in their face and their breath may be shallow, or they may even be holding your breath, bracing with fear. The illustration is not just an added bonus to make the book prettier; it's a vital part of helping readers' motor systems infer based on experiencing those same feelings in their own bodies.

As adults today worry about empathy gaps and children and teen's ability to have social imagination (i.e., to put themselves in someone else's shoes), the answer could be as simple as looking at one another more. We can't use our bodies to make inferences if we are not actually looking at one another. Taking more time to slow down, use less technology to communicate, and really look at each other's facial expressions and body language takes little time. Once the awkwardness subsides, it can become a more rewarding and connecting experience for students. Encourage students to develop awareness and make looking at others a habit.

In this photo, high school students act out what they are envisioning in the scene they are reading. As long as a few brave students agree to try acting, their peers are more likely to give it a try. After the awkwardness goes away, students often ask to get up and move.

WHAT TYPES OF MOVEMENT SUPPORT UNDERSTANDING?

Now that we know that movement is an important element in comprehension, let's look at what types of movements we want to incorporate into the classroom. If you have ever tried Readers Theater in your classroom, you have likely seen the positive results. A meta-analysis on the impact of Readers Theater showed it had a 1.23 effect size. Anything larger than 0.4 is considered effective. It has been shown to create more than a year's worth of growth (Mastrothanasis et al., 2023). It is not just because students like to act out scenes and view the activity as fun, although that does contribute to its success. One of the reasons Readers Theater is a useful teaching tool is because it acknowledges the role that movement plays in developing comprehension.

Think about any young child you have been around during and after reading at home. They almost can't help but gesture, move their bodies, and then pretend they are the topic or character they just read about. Much of early childhood self-directed play stems from the stories students are exposed to. But, this playful movement is not just beneficial for young children. Countless studies with college students show that movement is an important element of comprehension to help students process information, make inferences, fill in gaps, understand abstract concepts, and think creatively.

Different types of movement support different kinds of comprehension across contexts and texts. In this section we will focus on five types of movement and their connection to students' understanding. For the purposes of simplifying language and making the research more accessible, I renamed each type of movement in more everyday terms that can be used in planning and teaching. You'll see them referred to as matching movement, goal-directed movement, experience movement, stepping in movement, and comparison movement. Each type can help us understand how students learn to comprehend language (both oral and written).

Matching Movement

Matching movements are known in the research as congruent movements. This type of movement means it aligns directly to the concept. For example, a matching movement would be acting out throwing a ball to represent the phrase "Throw me the ball." In a math classroom, matching movement might be used to introduce the concept of a number line and how numbers work along it. Students could line up across the room with numbers written on pieces of paper on the floor. When asked to take one small step to add one, they would physically move to the next number. When asked to take a larger leap, up three numbers, they would make a larger movement with their bodies to add three. Research with addition and subtraction being taught this way has shown that connecting numbers with movements leads to later math knowledge and skill (Link et al., 2014). In a reading situation, matching movement might include reading the sentence "Ethan chased the cat" while running in place. Another example might include reading about a swimming technique while simulating the same movement you just read about.

The Moved by Reading studies, conducted by Arthur Glenberg and his colleagues, used matching movement to support reading comprehension. In one of his studies he asked first and second graders to read a short passage about farm life. Half of the students in the study were given farm toys such as a barn, tractor, and cow. Periodically a light would turn on and students were asked to either reread or act out the story using the toys. After the reading, the group of students who were asked to act out the story were better able to remember details from the story and make inferences compared to their peers who were only asked to reread. Acting out a story boosted students' understanding by fifty percent compared to those who simply reread (Glenberg et al., 2004). In similar studies with reading math problems, Glenberg and his colleagues found that acting out the math problem's story helped students identify information that was important for the solution.

Having students perform matching movements activated the motor aspects of the brain. This motor activation was later tested in other studies when people simply read the words without physically acting them out. They found that the same parts of the brain, the motor system, are activated when reading the word *kick* as when physically kicking. "Modern neuroscience has yet to find anything like an abstract, completely isolated reading area of the brain. Rather, when we read, we tend to activate the same sensory and motor brain areas involved in doing what we are reading about" (S. Beilock, 2015, p. 50). This means that reading comprehension is at least in part tied to our motor system, not just when we are infants but throughout life.

Matching movements are not simply about understanding individual words devoid of context. The *indexical hypothesis* claims that words are indexed to objects; for example, the word *cup* is indexed by the cup on the table. The actions made available by those objects are referred to as affordances; for example, sipping and pouring are affordances of the cup. Affordances allow us to process language by simulating the same neural mechanism that is used in our real-world actions and perceptions (Glenberg & Robertson, 2000). If we break this jargon down a bit, it simply means that the movement associated with an object (whether we move it or perceive the movement done by others) activates the motor system in our brains. These possible movements, which are called affordances, support the idea that language is understood in our bodies just like when we actually sip or pour from the cup. "Language understanding is grounded in bodily action" (Glenberg & Kaschak, 2002, p. 562). This means it is tremendously helpful for students to understand what something is, where it is, and what possible uses or affordances it offers. These understandings initiate movement and comprehension.

In additional studies in the Moved by Reading approach, the researchers removed the toys that were used for acting out the passage. Instead, the students were asked to imagine manipulating the toys. They used the phrase "imagine manipulating the toys" because it was directly related to the actual movement the students had previously done and it made the directions clear. Again, students in the group that were asked to imagine the movement made huge gains in comprehension. This held true with third and fourth graders who read new stories, not just the ones they had previously read with the toys in hand (Marley et al., 2010).

As soon as children have some action experience, they can imagine performing the action in the stories and get the same benefits of physical movement. This concept of being able to comprehend language by activating the movement in our motor system is also referred to as *simulation theory.* It is when our brains simulate the actions we read about as if we were performing them ourselves.

S. Beilock (2015) explains, "Just as when we read the word *kick* and the foot area of the motor cortex comes alive, acting out a sentence helps us connect words and their referents. Children can link what they are reading explicitly to the actions and events the words describe" (p. 52). This insight helps us make the research a bit more practical. We can make more space in our classrooms for matching movement. This might mean we include more Readers Theater in whole group reading experiences. We can also consider making comprehension manipulatives available for students of all ages to help them when reading in small groups or independently.

What I mean by comprehension manipulatives is a set of concrete tools that students of any age can use to simulate the content of their readings. These manipulatives can also be used to organize, plan, and revise writing as well.

Comprehension Manipulatives (Appendix O)

Manipulative	How Students Might Use Them
Play dough	Create models, artifacts, and scenes Make comparisons of size, shape, and distance of objects created Represent pressure and tension, and experience sensory input that matches relationships
Sticky notes (variety of sizes and shapes)	Sequence events by using each sticky note to represent an event Organize information into categories with one piece of information per sticky note
Blocks	Build ideas by stacking blocks to represent each idea Construct settings that character manipulatives can move within
Figurines	Act out character movements Represent character interactions and relationships Role play scenes

Manipulative	How Students Might Use Them
Legos	Construct models Show connections between concepts and ideas with different brick colors, sizes, and shapes Make comparisons with each brick representing one unit/idea/concept
Popsicle sticks	Keep track of quantities Use them as pointers Build bridges between other manipulatives
Paper clips	Track quantities Build connections Use them as props when figurines reenact scenes

Goal-Directed Movement

While it can be easy to understand how matching movement helps us understand language because it directly matches the words being read, abstract language that does not have a direct movement match can be a bit more complex. Take, for example, the sentence from the first page of the book *The Outsiders* by Hinton (1967). The sentence reads, "I was wishing I looked like Paul Newman—he looks tough and I don't—but I guess my own looks aren't so bad" (p. 1). The verb *wishing* doesn't really correlate to a specific movement and is a much more abstract concept than verbs like *sipping* and *kicking*.

To understand this sentence, the student can use goal-directed movement, that is, movement that does not directly match the words and instead connects the words to the goal. The student has to understand that the subject of this sentence has a goal to be more tough looking. Once we identify the goal, we can still imagine movement the speaker would make that matches the goal. For example, you might picture the speaker puffing up his chest, making his shoulders broad, and standing with his legs apart. These movements do not directly match the text's words but do connect the words in the text to the goal of the character. You can see how the abstract concept of wishing still has a motor component to it when we picture the goal-directed movement.

The Noices, the same researchers mentioned in the section about memory and movement, describe this sort of goal-directed movement as a form of "reverse engineering." They discovered this process by studying the ways actors use goal-directed movement in the theater. They found that actors get a script, which mostly includes dialogue, and they have to figure out the goal of each line. As they determine the goal the character has, based on the words they say, they create movements to connect the two. For example, the researchers studied actors in the play *Cat on a Hot Tin Roof* and noted that when the character of Big Daddy's wife sat down next to Big Daddy, he said, "I need a little river breeze," while getting up and moving across the room to the open French doors. To comprehend what was going on, the actor had to read the dialogue, identify the character's goal (to get some distance from his wife), and then choose movements that would connect the two (walking to the open door). This goal-directed movement of getting distance from his wife aids with comprehension of the line about needing a breeze, and the concept of what the phrase really means becomes more apparent.

Researchers found that "when verbal utterances and movements are connected, not literally as in the usual enactment effect, but at a higher order goal level, superior retention results" (Noice & Noice, 2001). This finding about oral language comprehension has implications for reading text as well. The researchers found that actors work backward from the words to the reasons why the words were stated, and then imagine the accompanying movement. Readers seem to do the same thing. They read the words, make inferences about the goals of the words, and then create movement in their minds to connect it.

How do we teach students to use goal-directed movement to understand more abstract ideas? First, students already have experience doing this; they just don't know they are doing it. Take, for example, the character Elsa in the movie *Frozen* singing, "The cold never bothered me anyway." There is no real matching movement to understand this phrase of "bothering me." Instead, children can picture Elsa lifting her chin, stretching her arms out wide as she lets her cape fly off of her back. A smile grows across her face. These movements helped the movie watchers connect the words and the goals to truly comprehend the abstract idea of her being proud of who she really is and not wanting to hide it anymore. From watching TV, movies, and people in their lives, students come to learning experiences already having had successful experiences with goal-directed movement to aid in comprehension.

Some students, especially those who are neurodivergent, may not enter school with these skills mastered. If this is the case with some of your students, you can explicitly teach students how to make these sorts of inferences.

HELP STUDENTS INFER WITH GOAL-DIRECTED MOVEMENTS

1. Read the sentence(s).
2. Think about the goal of the words.
3. Act out or picture a movement that connects the words to the goals.

It may take modeling, guided practice, and repeated coaching for students to grasp this concept. Offer low-stakes opportunities across texts and topics until students start to understand and apply the process on their own. Of course, adjust expectations and strategies.

Classroom Practices That Support Goal-Directed Movement

Practice	Description
Reverse engineer	Students read a short part of a story and think about the goal of the passage. Then they act them out, noticing what movements they make. Variation: Do this with mental imagery and simulate in your head instead of acting.
Mute button	Students pair up. One partner reads a short part of a story, thinks about the goal of that part, and then acts out that part without saying anything. The watching partner has not read the passage and tries to use what they saw to guess the goal based on seeing the movements made. (Note: Readers do not guess the actual words or plot, just the goal. E.g., She wanted to run away or he needed to pump himself up.)
Gesture	Students read a short nonfiction passage or excerpt from one. They think about the goal of the lines they read. Then they use hand movements to connect the goal to the information. For example, after reading the sentence "The snake slithered under a rock to take cover," the student can use one hand to show the slithering movement and the other hand to be a rock it goes under.

Experience Movement

As students grow older and begin to read about much more abstract concepts such as those in physics and philosophy, movement still has an important role to play. The ability to feel a sensation in your own body through a new experience helps with understanding and application of information. Many of the studies done in this area were conducted by S. L. Beilock and Fischer (2013) with students learning physics.

Because the study of physics requires students to read and understand concepts like angular velocity and centrifugal force without a felt sense of what they are like, decades of research have found that many students never really grasp the concepts. In fact, studies found that "students' understanding of physics becomes less accurate after they completed an introductory physics course" (Paul, 2021, p. 60). This was due to traditional methods of teaching physics by treating students' brains like computers and asking them to solve problems by applying abstract concepts they didn't really understand. One reason why this method was not working is because "humans solve problems most effectively by imagining themselves into a given scenario," which is much easier if you have had some previous physical experience (Paul, 2021, p. 60).

A series of studies designed by S. L. Beilock and Fischer (2013) were conducted with physics students at DePaul University. Participants were given opportunities to experience physics concepts in their bodies. For example, in one study, two bicycle wheels were mounted on a single axle, which was held out from the body. The wheels were spun horizontally and then vertically and the students were able to physically feel torque in their own bodies. Torque is the force that causes objects to rotate. During this study, half the students had the experience of holding the wheels and feeling the torque while the other half had the experience of watching the demonstration of it. They found that the students who had the physical experience of torque with their own bodies achieved higher scores on the assessment of understanding than those who simply observed. The results also showed up in their ability to answer very challenging theoretical questions.

In a later part of the study, students' brains were studied in fMRI machines. The students who had the direct experience of torque in their bodies showed the movement areas of their brains were activated but not in those who only observed the torque wheel model. This finding has major implications for the use of movement and also the limitations of demonstration. The researchers found, "When demonstrations are incorporated . . . students should not be relegated to the role of observer. Only those who physically participate will gain the deeper, from-the-inside understanding that comes from physical action" (Paul, 2021, p. 61). This means as teachers who model for students, we need to recognize that after every model, students need time to do the work themselves. Watching us do the work is not enough. This makes sense given the robust effects of guided practice on student learning.

PLAN FOR EXPERIENCE MOVEMENT

In this lesson I invited students to experience a shift in perspective by looking through a small opening they made in their hand. This was meant to offer experience with the abstract concept of perspective.

1. Identify the abstract concept students will need to understand.
2. Ask yourself, "What movement could help students experience this concept?"
3. Model, but then offer time for students to try it themselves.

Consider offering explicit modeling and practice for students to feel in their bodies what some abstract concepts are like. The following table lists some common learning concepts, types of movements, and examples. When in doubt, try it yourself and see what movements help you *feel* the concept in your own body.

Movements That Teach Abstract Concepts

Concept	Movement	Example to Try
State of mind	Open or closed	Open and close a door Lay down with arms open and wide and then curl up in a ball
Passage of time	Forward or back	Step forward or backward
Motivation	Push (toward) or pull (away)	Push your hands against a wall Try pulling an object toward you
Conflict	Separation	Partially tear a paper
Confusion	Dizziness and disorientation	Nod your head "no" vigorously (and safely) and then feel the dizzying effect
Relationship	Connection, disconnection	Hold hands with someone and then have one person let go
Perspective	Narrow vision or wide angle vision	Make a small circle with your hand to look through and then use peripheral vision without anything in your way
Hierarchy	Up or down	Crouch down and stand up tall

Stepping in Movement

Recall how earlier in the chapter I described the ways we envision, either as a participant or an observer. When we imagine ourselves into the text as a participant, as if we are doing the movement ourselves, this is known as self-referential movement. I call this "stepping in movement" because it is as if we stepped into the scene, setting, or topic and are along for the ride. It is like a form of empathy where we "bring ourselves—in particular, our bodies—into the intellectual enterprise" (Paul, 2021, p. 61). Many famous and well respected scientists describe the ways they use this stepping in movement to help them make discoveries and understand concepts. For example, Nobel Prize–winning geneticist Barbara McClintock is quoted as saying,

"When I was really working with them [chromosomes], I wasn't outside. I was down there. I was part of the system. I was right down there with them and everything got big . . . . It surprised me because I actually felt as if I were right down there and these were my friends" (as quoted in Paul, 2021, p. 61).

Virologist Jonas Salk, who invented the polio vaccine, said, "I would picture myself as the virus or a cancer cell, for example, and try to sense what it would be like to be either. I would also imagine myself as the immune system" (Paul, 2021, p. 62). Albert Einstein, the most famous theoretical physicist, was quoted as saying, "No scientist thinks in equations," and that their thoughts were "visual and even muscular in nature" (p. 62). He explained that he imagined himself on the beam of light while developing the theory of relativity.

So what does this have to do with teaching students to comprehend as they read? We can employ this "embodied imagination" just like scientists do. In one study done at the University of Washington (Scherr et al., 2013), a professor created what she called an Energy Theater to help students use this stepping in movement to understand what they were reading about. In this role playing experience, students didn't just read about energy conservation in their textbook but also used movement to embody the energy. Dr. Scherr, the professor, found that her students developed a more nuanced understanding of energy dynamics from this sort of stepping in movement as if they were the energy themselves.

Similarly, Joseph Chinnici at the Virginia Commonwealth University found that his students better understood biology concepts they read about after acting out the processes with their own bodies. Students who had engaged in role playing as if they were the cells participating in mitosis and meiosis had a more accurate understanding of the concepts. In multiple studies "students learned more and performed better when they were offered the opportunity to embody these entities rather than simply reading or hearing about them" (Paul, 2021, p. 63).

A series of studies from Professor Smith at the University of Vermont found that students "learn even more when the manipulatives they employ are their brown bodies" (Paul, 2021, p. 64). This finding came from studies where students physically embodied concepts. Smith claims that "being it—embodying a conceptual object—is a very different experience from watching it, or viewing a conceptual object as remote and separate from oneself" (p. 64). The following chart lists ways to incorporate this stepping in movement into the literacy classroom.

Stepping In Movement Classroom Practices

Stepping in Experience	Description	Example
Personify	**Be it:** Take some time to make your body match the concept, character, setting, or topic you are reading about.	After reading about land formations, make your body into them. Be a peninsula, be an island, etc.
Role Play	**Move like it:** Become the character or topic of your reading and then move like they would move. Act it out as if you were the topic.	While reading about how lava flows out of a volcano, become the lava. Make movements to match what the lava is doing.
Shape Shift in Your Mind	**Imagine it:** Pause your reading to step into the text and be a part of the topic. Turn your body into the topic in your mind.	Imagine yourself as the flame burning on the hearth. You have become the fiery flame yourself in your mind's eye.

Comparison Movement

A final type of movement, comparison movement, is often referred to in the research as metaphorical movement. This sort of movement is tied to the studies conducted by Lakoff and Johnson (1980). They found that much of our language is metaphorical and connects to movement and bodies. Some of the many examples include the following:

- When someone is happy, we say they are "up" or "flying high."
- When some is sad, we say they are "down in the dumps."
- People "hit rock bottom."
- After making a choice, we may say we "can't turn back now."
- When ideas are "flowing," we are "on a roll."

These metaphors "reveal the way people represent and think about abstract concepts, and importantly, those representations result from literal interactions of the body with the world. When people are sad they literally slump, sit or lie down, whereas when someone is joyous, they carry themselves erect and may literally jump for joy" (Glenberg & Gallese, 2012, p. 587). In many ways, the Lakoff and Johnson (1980) work, *Metaphors We Live By*, began the research movement toward embodiment and how our bodies are involved in comprehension. There is a reciprocity where the metaphors shape how we experience, the world and also the ways we experience the world create the metaphors.

Comparison movement is the ability to understand texts by enacting the movement described in the metaphor in our own motor system and using the feeling associated with it to infer meaning. For example, in *Diary of a Wimpy Kid*, by Kinney (2007), the character says, "I guess I kind of felt sorry for Rowley, and I decided to take him under my wing" (p. 19). Students can understand what this phrase "take him under my wing" means because they know the feeling and goal associated with the movement. It could be acted out as if our arm is a wing, or students could imagine the movement in their minds to get a sense of the feeling being implied. It is clear that the character under the wing is being taken care of and is also smaller than the one with the wing. By noting the feeling and the size, it allows the student to infer the relationship between the two (who is higher up in the hierarchy) and the goal of the character speaking to offer protection and care.

A simple way to support students with comparison movement is for them to pause, move, and ponder when they encounter a metaphor. The following chart shows what the process may look like in the classroom.

Pause-Move-Ponder Practice

Steps	Example from *Class Act*, by Jerry Craft
1. **Pause** when you come to a metaphor or comparison.	"But after school, knock yourself out" (p. 30).
2. **Move** your body to match the metaphor.	Pretend to knock yourself in the head and fall over.
3. **Ponder.** What feeling is associated with the movement? How does this connect back to the text?	I am laid out on the floor and cannot move. Totally still. It means they can do what they want outside of school, as much as they want, to the point of total exhaustion.

The ways we move our body impact the ways we think, so when someone wants to think creatively, it can be helpful to physically move our bodies in a creative way. In one study undertaken by psychologist Evan Polman, he asked students to complete a creative thinking task. One group of students was asked to complete the task while sitting in a large five-foot-square cardboard box to replicate "thinking inside the box." The other group of students was asked to do the same task while seated outside and next to the box. The students who were literally seated outside the box came up with a list of creative ideas that was twenty percent longer than the group in the box (Leung et al., 2012).

In another study Polman and his colleagues (Leung et al., 2012) asked students to come up with creative ideas for the use of a new campus building complex. They used the metaphor "on the one hand and on the other hand" to guide their study of multiple possibilities. One group of students was asked to hold out one hand as they brainstormed ideas. The other group was asked to alternate between holding out one hand and then the other as they brainstormed. The students did not receive any information about why they were asked to hold out hands and were not told the metaphor being used by the researchers. Findings showed that the group who alternated between the one and the other came up with fifty percent more potential uses for the buildings than the other group who only held up one hand. A group of independent judges also found the group with the alternating hands to have come up with more varied and creative ideas. They found that "embodying metaphors for creativity appears to help ignite the engine of creativity" (p. 7).

While the practicality of asking students to physically enact metaphors all day long is not reasonable, we can learn from comparison movements and consider its use in our classrooms. Since we know that we often communicate our understanding of complex ideas in comparisons, we can build this into our lessons. If we want students to infer character feelings, for example, using our bodies to act out the feelings and then comparing language to the action can be a helpful strategy. The following table illustrates some examples for using metaphors to describe our understanding of elements of a text. Students can start with movement and then put a metaphor to it, or they can begin with the metaphor and then enact the movement that goes with it. No matter if you start with the comparison or the movement, just make sure to include both.

In addition to using comparison and movement to better understand elements of a text, you can also use comparison to generate more creative thinking. Try out the "on the one hand and on the other hand" experience by asking students to alternate between holding up each hand while discussing creative ideas with one another. One example I have used with students of all ages is the Elephant and Piggie book *Let's Go for a Drive*, by Willems (2017). After spending the entire book collecting items they will need for a drive, the characters realize they do not have the most important item, the car. I ask students, "How could they solve this problem?" In just a few minutes students generate long lists of creative, if not realistic, options. A few examples of their ideas include the following:

- Call their mom.
- Hire an Uber.
- Steal a car.

- Make roller skates out of their luggage and skate instead.
- Use their luggage as a pretend car and just make believe play instead.
- Use their umbrella to invent a flying machine.

By prompting students to think creatively and use their bodies to embody a metaphor like "on the one hand and on the other," you can engage students in deep thinking.

PROMPTS FOR THINKING CREATIVELY

- How else could the conflict have been resolved?
- What other choices did the character have?
- What other reactions could that character have had?
- What if a character was not included in the story? How would it have changed the plot?
- Which perspectives were missing in this text? Name as many as you can.
- What if the setting were different? Think of as many other settings as possible and how they would impact the story.

A LOOK IN THE MIRROR

Multiple studies on how walking impacts people's thinking have shown that walking leads to more creative outcomes than sitting still (Paul, 2021).

In one study of creative thinking, participants were asked to generate unexpected uses for everyday objects. The group who spent their time walking while thinking generated on average four to six more uses than the group who remained seated (Oppezzo & Schwartz, 2014).

College professors and dissertation advisors have begun asking students to go for walks during class instead of the traditional sit and listen lecture (Paul, 2021).

Try out "walk and talks."

Notice how often your own thinking gets stale and stuck when you have been sitting for too long. You can also benefit from movement when planning for instruction and bringing more creativity into your teaching.

- Consider walking with colleagues for reflection and planning time.
- If you want to be more creative, find a meandering free-form route and do not follow a set path or agree on an end point ahead of time.
- Notice your feelings and the ways your thoughts flow while walking.

Metaphor and Movement Examples

Story Element	Possible Metaphors	Possible Movements	Meaning
Characters	They need to let off steam.	Jump up and push your hands overhead	Angry and need to let it out
	They feel the weight of the world on their shoulders.	Slumped down and shoulders rounded	Pressured and stressed
	Energy is bubbling over.	Pop up and down	Excited and it is building
	They are light as a feather.	Smiling and resting Lying down	Carefree
	She has nerves of steel.	Stand up tall and solid and unmoving with a straight face	Courageous
Relationships	He is a rock.	Sit solid and grounded and unmoving	Secure and stable
	This is like a rollercoaster.	Move up and down like a rollercoaster	Full of surprises and lots of change
	They are each other's missing puzzle piece.	Two hands joining together and fitting in place.	Complementing each other and completing one another
Themes	There is light at the end of the tunnel.	Squinting into darkness	Hope is coming because . . .
	The key to happiness is . . .	Putting a key into a lock	The missing element is . . .
	The pathway toward . . .	Walk down a path	The logical conclusion is . . .

The following table summarizes the types of movements discussed in this chapter.

TYPES OF MOVEMENT SUMMARY CHART (APPENDIX P)

Type of Movement	Meaning	Example
Matching Movement	When the movement directly matches the words	Acting like a bunny hopping while reading about a bunny hopping
Goal-Directed Movement	When the movement does not directly match the words but is connected by a goal the words convey	Inferring the character's motivation and making a facial expression and body movement to show what the character wants (even though those actions are not described in the text)
Experience Movement	When movement introduces us to an abstract concept through a bodily experience	Understanding character relationships by tapping into your feeling of connection and disconnection
Stepping in Movement	When you imagine yourself in the text and move as if you are the topic being read about	Reading about how the water cycle works by acting as if you are a water molecule and imagining the journey of movement you would take
Comparison Movement	When you use movement to understand language by the feeling the movement brings	When reading about a character as "a force of nature," using the feeling of natural forces like large wind gusts to get an understanding of what the character was like—the feeling of the movement the language implies

A SUMMARY OF KEY IDEAS FROM CHAPTER 5

This chapter examined movement's influence on understanding. We learned how our motor systems influence our memory, both procedural and declarative, and help students develop literal and inferential comprehension through performing and watching different kinds of movement.

- Movement plays a key role in memory for both teachers and students.
- Reading skills across the content area, such as envisioning and making inferences, are often connected to our motor system and can be accessed through intentional movement or mental simulation.
- Five types of movement support language comprehension. They include matching, goal-directed, experience, stepping in, and comparison movements.
- You can incorporate movement experiences into what you are already teaching to enhance students' comprehension and spark their creativity.

A SUMMARY OF PRACTICES FROM CHAPTER 5

Practices	Reflection Questions	When and Where I May Use This
Add movement into classroom procedures (page 114).	Which procedures do students struggle to remember? How might I add in a movement to help?	
Create memory tags by adding movement into memorization (page 117).	What is worth students' time committing to memory? How might we work together to create movements to help?	
Add movement into envisioning lessons (page 119).	Which texts or parts of texts that I teach would be hard to envision? Which movements could I include to support the pictures in students' minds?	
Support social imagination with facial expressions (page 122).	Where can I naturally fit in social imagination lessons? What kinds of conversations might I have with students about the importance of looking at one another?	
Make comprehension manipulatives available and show students how to use them (page 128).	What kind of modeling of these manipulatives would my students benefit from seeing? What routines do I need to put in place to make sure students are not simply playing with them in distracted ways?	

Practices	Reflection Questions	When and Where I May Use This
Add goal-directed movements into inference lessons (page 131).	How do I want to describe goal-directed inferences to my students? Where are they already doing this work? How might I add in more movement to make it more concrete?	
Try out reverse engineer, mute button, and gesture partner activities (page 132).	Where in my curriculum or with which texts might these activities support students?	
Introduce abstract concepts with movements (page 135).	Which abstract concepts do my students need help understanding?	
Try out personify, role play, and shape shift activities (page 137).	Where in my curriculum or with which texts might these activities support students?	
Try the pause-move-ponder practice (page 139).	How can I make this strategy a routine students can revisit many times as needed?	
Develop some prompts for thinking creatively (page 142).	What sorts of creative thinking do I want to support in students? Which prompts can I use right away to get started?	

Chapter 6 Students Use Gestures to Create and Communicate Understanding

"Gestures give life to our mental scratch pads."

— Sian Beilock

PRIME YOURSELF

Take a moment to talk to someone face-to-face about your predictions before beginning to read this chapter. As you talk, notice what your hands are doing.

- Do you find yourself pointing or moving your hands in any directions?
- Are the gestures small or large, fast or slow?
- Also notice what your speaking partner's gestures look like. When do they gesture?
- How are you using their hand movements to listen, stay engaged, or understand what they are saying?

When we pay attention to other peoples' gestures, not only are we developing understanding of their words and ideas but also we are more able to read their emotions. Having this awareness of gesture offers you another level of potential understanding of yourself and others.

In this chapter we will build on the previous chapter's focus on the role movement plays in developing comprehension across content areas. We will zoom in on the role gesture plays when we are teaching and when students are learning and trying to communicate that learning to others.

WHAT ARE THE BENEFITS OF GESTURES?

Take a look around the classroom, and notice how even though you may be too far away to hear what students are saying to one another, you can get a lot of information from watching their gestures. You can infer their tone by noticing big or small hand movements. You can also infer their purpose, that is, to figure something out or share something. You can even infer the meaning—conveying events or explaining ideas. Gesturing has at least two important functions for comprehension: to facilitate understanding and to communicate that understanding to others.

As teachers, we also use gestures in both intentional and unintentional ways. Sometimes we use gestures to accompany the "teacher look" and communicate to students that they should stop what they are doing, even without having to use words. Oftentimes, we use gestures when explaining and modeling, and the hand movements become a complementary form of communication that both mirrors and extends what our words convey.

Moving our bodies with gestures enhances memory. When we gesture while we speak, we are creating what are called mental "hooks" that enable students to "reel" in the information later when needed (S. Beilock, 2015). Beilock explains, "When it is time to remember, you have two hooks (one related to action and one to speech) with which to fish out the information" (p. 92). Traditionally, we suggest students make acronyms and use other language-based means to memorize. While this can be helpful, we know that adding in gestures and movement can have a larger impact on memory and retention. Encourage students to use both language and movement when committing things to memory.

Researchers who study embodied cognition have found that "people formulate and convey their thoughts not only with words but also with motions of the hands and the body. Gestures don't merely echo or amplify spoken language; they carry out cognitive and communicative functions that language can't touch" (Paul, 2021 p. 69). These cognitive functions help the person doing the gestures and the watcher of the gestures.

Benefits for the Person Doing the Gesturing	Benefits for the Person Watching the Gestures
• Offload information into our hands that frees up more mental space • Helps with understanding abstract ideas • Helps process spatial and relational concepts • Helps us work through confusions and captures some of our emerging understanding • More persuasive and memorable to intended audience • Communicates feelings and creates tone • Creates a "visual hook"	• Enhances memory • Reinforces key ideas and points • Aids in understanding someone's overall idea • Helps fill in gaps in the other person's speech • Can become a preview of concepts that have not been conveyed in words • Helps listener infer someone else's feelings

You may be wondering what I mean by gesturing. Some of us may think of gestures in terms of the emotional middle finger gesture used by teenagers to show others they need space. We may be picturing our young child blowing us a kiss, showing us an endearing moment of affection. In fact, there are several types of gestures that people use both in and out of school to make sense of their world and communicate with others. The following table (see page 153) summarizes the main types of gestures and examples of what this might look like in a classroom. This table was developed as I synthesized the work of Paul (2021) and Kita and Emmorey (2023).

Types of Gesture Summary Chart (Appendix Q)

Type	Description	Example
Iconic	Used to depict movement, action, and shape	Moving arms in running motion like the character
Metaphorical	Used to depict abstract concepts	Moving hand from left to right to represent the passage of time when retelling
Deictic	Pointing gestures	Pointing at a picture of a character on the page
Emblem	Used in place of a word	Thumbs-up sign to signal the word *OK* during a book club conversation
Pragmatic	Communicate interactions	Shrugging shoulders to show lack of interest or uncertainty when asked a question
Beat	Hand moves up and down creating a sort of rhythm	Pumping a fist up and down to emphasize points and draw attention when in a debate

Let's examine two main purposes of gestures and how we can tap their power to help students develop and share their thinking. We'll look at practical applications for both students and teachers.

HOW DO STUDENTS USE GESTURES TO DEVELOP UNDERSTANDING?

Researcher Susan Goldin-Meadow explains that "gesture encourages experimentation" (quoted in Jaffe, 2004). This is because we tend to gesture profusely when we are first trying to figure something out. As we process new information that is unfamiliar to us, we tend to gesture much more than when we have already figured it out. We also tend to gesture more when there is a challenge and that challenge has many possibilities. We gesture more when "so cognitively demanding is the task of assimilating a new idea that we divide the work between our head and our hands, each going its own way for now" (Paul, 2021, p. 76). Researchers call this "muddled talk" because of the lack of clarity (Roth & Lawless, 2002).

The act of gesturing tends to help us develop insight and more understanding. Psychologist Tversky (2019) calls this a "virtual diagram" we create in the air with our gestures that help us both stabilize and advance our understanding. These virtual diagrams help students come to some solid conclusions and begin to organize their thoughts.

In one study, people were asked to write about a complex topic. One group was allowed to talk and gesture before writing and the other was told not to. The group that was not allowed to talk and gesture was found to have less astute reasoning and draw fewer inferences (Walkington et al., 2014). Gesture assists us with grappling with complex ideas.

In another study, college science professors video recorded conversations in their lab when they were trying to figure out how a blood protein functioned. The video recordings revealed the ways the professor and graduate students who worked in the lab collaboratively developed a series of gestures as they discussed their theories. They used their hands as symbols, pointed, and added movement. These gestures were a huge part of helping them create their new knowledge. They found that gestures were essential in their comprehension process (Becvar et al., 2005).

A LOOK IN THE MIRROR

Some of us more naturally use gestures than others. Based on your cultural and familial identity, you may have had lots of modeling of gestures or been told not to move your hands so much. Research has found that when children see adults gesturing, they tend to make more hand movements themselves (Paul, 2021). You can both explicitly tell students that gestures are beneficial and also encourage them to use gestures as they talk and teach one another.

Practice this yourself first. The next time you sit down to talk with a colleague, tell them you want to practice using intentional gestures. Then try out some of the strategies in this section. It may feel awkward and you may be self-conscious at first, but like anything new, you get used to it.

On the other hand (eye roll for this pun), if you are someone who already uses lots of gestures, ask a colleague to give you some feedback. What do they notice about when and how you use gestures? Try to be more self-aware and bring more consciousness to your hand movements. Too much movement in a constant fashion may become distracting. For some people, like myself, it can help to use a little restraint and decide when to gesture and when not to.

Finally, notice that you may gesture more or less based on your own understanding and emotions around the topic you are teaching about. Do you gesture more when you are talking or teaching about a new concept? Do certain kinds of interactions lead to more gestures? Self-reflection on our gestures offers us a doorway into deeper understanding of our own thinking and teaching.

For young children who are still developing oral language, gestures are a main communication tool. Children's new and emerging ideas about concepts tend to be expressed in gestures before they even attempt to put words to them. My own son used pointing gestures as a baby to request items long before he had the oral language to verbally ask for them. This is sometimes the case for anyone who is learning a new language. Many students who enter school in the earliest stages of English language acquisition tend to use gestures to communicate as their English oral language develops.

Formative Assessment. As teachers, we can pay attention to students' gestures as an important piece of information about their understanding. When we only pay attention to students' words, we are missing so much of their process and possibly also their thinking. Goldin-Meadow (2005) found that there are three look-fors when it comes to students' gestures and understanding. When looking at gestures and listening to language at the same time you can notice when (a) gestures and speech match and are correct, (b) gestures and speech match but are incorrect, or (c) gestures do not match speech.

- When gestures and speech match and are correct, students' movements are called congruent, and this is interpreted as a sign of understanding.
- When gestures and speech match and are incorrect, students' movements signal they are far from understanding.
- When there is a mismatch between gestures and speech, students' movements are considered transitional and show movement from the incorrect words to the correct expression in gesture. They are getting closer to fully understanding.

Researchers Church and Goldin-Meadow (1986) recorded videos of children performing conservation tasks, which test a child's ability to see that some properties are conserved as an object undergoes physical transformation such as water being poured from a tall skinny glass to a short and wide glass. They found that understanding first emerged as gesture, before speech, forty percent of the time. In another study, fifteen-year-olds were observed performing a problem-solving task. They found that there was a mismatch between speech and gesture thirty-two percent of the time (Church & Goldin-Meadow, 1986). These mismatches show the teachers that students are ready for instruction. When teachers recognize the mismatch, they can view it as an opportunity because it means teaching is more likely to stick. This reminds me of the wisdom that Donald Bear shared in his Words Their Way program that we know students are ready for our teaching when they are "using but confusing" concepts.

Quick Formative Assessment Tool for Capturing Understanding (Appendix R)

Student ______________________ Focus ______________________

What I See	Evidence	What It Might Mean
Gesture-Speech Match Correct Understanding		Student understands and does not need instruction
Gesture-Speech Match Incorrect Understanding		Student does not yet understand and may need more time and experience
Gesture-Speech Mismatch		Student is moving toward understanding and is ready for instruction

Instructional Next Steps:

Offloading: One theory of why and how people use gestures to process information centers on taking some of the load off our brains. S. Beilock (2015) explains, "When we gesture, some of what we are working on can virtually be held at our fingertips, freeing up our mind to hold other important pieces of information" (p. 89). In other words, moving our hands frees up brain power to do more thinking.

In studies of both children and adults who were asked to remember letters and words while performing a math problem, the participants used gestures to help them lighten the cognitive load. Both children and adults remembered significantly more items when they gestured during their explanations than when they did not. Researchers found that participants used gestures to save cognitive resources while performing the explanation task, so that they could allocate more resources to the memory task (Goldin-Meadow et al., 2001).

Simulation: A theory about why people gesture to develop understanding is tied back to our motor systems. S. Beilock (2015) explains, "Gestures give life to our mental scratch pads, allowing us to perform actions with our hands before we have to do them in real life or before we have thought these activities all the way through to put them into words. . . . Gestures are really just an outgrowth of how we might mentally simulate performing activities" (p. 90). Many studies show students using their hands to mentally rehearse or simulate the answer to a problem before they even put words to it. Athletes do this too. Watch any professional basketball game or golf tournament and notice how often the athlete physically simulates the shot or swing before doing it for real. This low-stakes rehearsal can be encouraged when students are working on a problem, trying to organize their thinking, or revising their thinking as they read. Anything that includes idea generation that is open-ended and complex could benefit from some gestural rehearsal before committing to an answer.

Foreshadowing: Research shows that we use gestures to foreshadow with our hands what we are about to say in words (Crowder, 1996). In fact, "our hands 'know' what we are about to say before our conscious minds do" (Paul, 2021, p. 72). Video studies show that our hands stop gesturing milliseconds before we stop talking when we say something in error. This foreshadowing effect also happens when we use gestures to prime our brains for the words to come. Studies show that when people are not able to gesture, their speech is less fluent and the words do not flow as easily (Pine et al., 2007). Notice how often you use gestures to help you with a word that is "right at the tip of your tongue."

The implications of using gestures to offload, rehearse, and prime mean we should encourage students to use gestures when they are learning and trying to remember. Many studies have found that teaching students to use gestures leads to more understanding and learning (Cook & Goldin-Meadow, 2006; Dargue & Sweller, 2020; Keehner & Gathercole, 2007; Son et al., 2018). The following table shows ideas for how you can explicitly teach students how to use gestures to develop their understanding.

How to Use Gestures to Develop Understanding (Appendix S)

Use Gestures to Understand When	Try Out	How a Listener Can Help
You are confused	Talk while using gestures and just let your hands move a lot. Allow ideas to flow through your hands. Don't worry about having it all make sense yet.	Have a listener be a mirror and share what they heard AND saw when you were talking.
You want to remember	Use your hands to offload information by using gestures to hold the information in a representational way for you.	Take notes on what you say and use them to help create a study guide.
You have partial understanding	Explain what you do know and then purposefully gesture about what you don't yet understand. Allow your hands to show the confusion.	Have a listener focus on the confusion and explain what they saw. Maybe they can pick up on some nuances of understanding you are not yet consciously aware of.
You feel like you understand but don't have the words yet to explain it	Use gestures to show what you know and let the words follow. Don't pay as much attention to the words yet and let the gesture take the place of words you don't yet have. Gestures can prime your brain for the words. You may be surprised that the words follow the gesture.	Have a listener name back and describe what they saw you gesture. Maybe they can help put words to the ideas you have, or they can simply listen as the words follow the gesture.

HOW CAN TEACHERS USE GESTURES?

Much of what we understand when others speak comes not just from listening but also from watching the other person's gestures. Research has shown the importance of oral language comprehension on successfully learning to read (Dickinson et al., 2010; Seidenberg, 2017). Much less attention has been focused on the research that gestures aid in oral language comprehension. For many of us teachers, gestures come out in unintentional ways or below our level of awareness, but we can more intentionally gesture while teaching. When we use gestures in purposeful ways, we invite students' brains to pay more attention and we are more likely to see an increase in comprehension.

Several research studies have shown that watching someone gesture

- creates greater attention,
- increases understanding of abstract concepts,
- improves memory,
- reduces cognitive load, and
- makes the speaker more persuasive.

In one study, people were thirty-three percent more likely to remember something they learned from a video if the content was connected to a gesture (Carlson et al., 2014).

The auditory cortex is activated when a person watches someone gesture while speaking. This area of the brain is responsible for processing oral language. Brain studies have shown that hand gestures appear to alert the auditory cortex that meaningful communication is occurring (Kelly et al., 2007). During video analysis of gestures and speech, researchers found that gestures help when speech is ambiguous or hard to understand. Both gestures that match and gestures that elaborate upon speech benefit the listeners (Dargue et al., 2019), especially when the concepts being spoken about are complex (McNeil et al., 2000).

All forms of gesture while teaching can enhance students' oral comprehension. Think of gestures as a moving visual aid you can use by simply using your hands. The following chart compares matching and elaborating gestures and lists when you may choose to use them.

Matching Gestures	Elaborating Gestures
The gesture matches the content of the spoken words. Choose to use this with • younger students who are still learning language, • multilingual learners who are acquiring English, • new concepts that may be difficult to understand, and • students who struggle to maintain focused attention.	**The gesture adds meaning to spoken words by including information that is not directly stated.** Choose to use this when you're teaching • abstract ideas such as motivation and internal conflict, • how the parts of what you are saying all connect by creating a visual diagram with your hands, • The relationship between parts (time passage, connections, hierarchy, etc.), and • something "dry" that could use some emotional connection to keep students' attention.

The table that follows offers examples of common skills you teach to students with accompanying gesture ideas you may want to try. Use this as an inspiration for creating your own set of gestures that match you and your students. These are called designed gestures because they are chosen ahead of time with intention.

Teacher Gestures When Modeling Skills (Appendix T)

Skills	When You Model and Say	Try These Gestures
Inferring	The character is feeling . . . 	Point to your facial expression, which matches the feeling. Make an emoji symbol with your hands and body (e.g., heart, point to wide eyes, shrug shoulders up).
Sequencing	First, then, next . . . 	Put up a finger as you say each sequence word like you are counting. Move your hand farther away from your body each time you say a new event to show them happening later in time.
Predicting	Because I already know _______, I think _______ will happen next. 	Point to head when you say, "I already know," and then point away from you to show prediction as you unfold your arm.

Synthesizing	If I put this detail and this detail together, it makes me think of this bigger idea that . . . 	Put up one fist for each idea and then clasp the hands together as you say the bigger idea that connects them.
Determining Importance	This detail is sort of small and not that important, but this one is really important because . . . 	Make a tiny pinching hand for a small detail and then expand your hand wide for the important detail. You can scrunch and open your eyes along with this too.
Envisioning	When I read this, I pictured . . . 	Point to your head as you close your eyes and describe the movie in your mind.

HOW CAN STUDENTS USE GESTURES TO SHARE THEIR LEARNING?

Gestures are not just a helpful tool for very young students. Michele Cooke, a geoscience professor who is hearing impaired, found that "repeated use of a structured system of meaning-bearing gestures helps improve spatial thinking" among her college students (Paul, 2022, p. 79). This research came from findings with both hearing and hearing impaired students who use American Sign Language. Cooke taught her students to use gestures as a modified form of sign language and found that it helped students understand the three-dimensional nature of the topics in her course. The professor now encourages students to use both speech and gestures in both systematic and more intuitive ways.

These findings are supported by studies conducted on penetrative thinking, which is the ability to visualize a three-dimensional object and "see" inside of it with your mind's eye. This skill is one in which many students, even at the college level, struggle. Students were originally tested in their ability to use penetrative thinking. Then one group was taught using just words while the other group was taught using words and gestures. The group that was taught using gestures scored significantly higher than their peers who only received words (Atit et al., 2018). So much of the content in a science class or the topic of a nonfiction text requires students to use penetrative thinking. We can use gestures to more effectively help with this skill. Some examples include understanding

- land formations,
- cellular biology,
- engineering and model building,
- envisioning inside of a building or room, and
- anatomy and our muscular skeletal system.

As students are reading or listening to a talk or video on these sorts of topics, pausing to use gestures can be especially helpful.

Recall from Chapter 5 about the power of metaphors when sharing thinking. Students can combine both metaphors and gestures when communicating their learning to others to boost their own comprehension and their listeners. Imagine first asking students to think of a comparison or metaphor and then to add a gesture to it when sharing it with others. When students are working with their peers and using gestures, Paul (2021) suggests, we can teach students by reminding them to "move your hands as you explain that" (p. 81).

The following chart can be created with students to teach them when and how to use gestures. Don't forget to frontload this teaching by explaining why gestures are important and to normalize the awkwardness that may present at first.

Use Gestures When Sharing

When I Am Sharing . . .	I May Gesture by . . .	Examples
My thoughts	Moving my hands to match what I am thinking	As you share your thinking about the story, use your hands to show your points.
My reactions	Using my facial expression to show a feeling or reaction	As you share your reaction, match your face to the reactions.
My learning	Creating a visual model with my hands to teach a concept I read about	As you teach us about this topic, use your hands to show us the parts.

Choose to prompt students to use gestures whenever they are sharing their understanding with others, whether it be you, a peer, or the class. You'll likely notice some students do this automatically without the need for a prompt, but many will benefit from it. You might say something like this to young students: "When you are sharing your learning with a partner, use your hands to SHOW them what you learned." With older students, you can explain the word *gestures* and the benefits of using them, and then say something like this: "Don't forget to include a gesture when talking to your partner. It will help them understand and remember your key ideas."

A SUMMARY OF KEY IDEAS FROM CHAPTER 6

In this chapter we looked at gesture and its role in both developing understanding and also sharing learning with others. Both teachers and students can benefit from using gestures to learn and to explain.

- Gestures help students develop understanding of new or complex concepts.
- Paying more attention to the role gestures already play in teaching and learning can help you leverage current strengths.
- Gestures give teachers insight into understanding that students' words alone may not show.
- Gestures help people communicate their understanding to others and create hooks that engage the listener.
- By choosing hand movements that show what you learned and what you think, you can more clearly communicate your understanding to others.

A SUMMARY OF PRACTICES FROM CHAPTER 6

Practice	Reflection Questions	When and Where I May Use This
Try the quick formative assessment tool for capturing understanding (page 157).	Who already uses gestures in your classroom? How might you use their gestures to deepen your curiosity and understanding of them?	
Teach students how to use gestures with partners to develop understanding (page 159).	How will you introduce the role of gestures to students who are acting as listening partners?	
Plan some intentional gestures when modeling skills (page 162).	How might you use more intentional gestures to help your teaching stick? Which abstract concepts would benefit from your using more gestures?	
Teach students how to use gestures when sharing with others (page 165).	What lessons might you teach students for when they share with peers? Which gestures will you introduce to them to try out?	

Chapter 7 Students Learn in Places

"All of us think differently depending on where we are. . . . [W]hile a laptop works the same whether it's being used at the office or we're sitting in the park, the brain is deeply affected by the setting in which it operates."

— Paul (2021, p. 92)

PRIME YOURSELF

As you begin reading this chapter there are three tips that can help you stay focused, boost happiness, and develop deeper understanding.

1. **Nature Awareness:** Take a moment to go outside, look out the window, or pull up a photo of a beautiful landscape. Spending a few minutes noticing nature can boost your attention, working memory, and concentration.
2. **Smile:** Take a pen and hold it in between your lips, forcing a smile. This hack allows your body to make your brain feel happier (and ready to read). It prepares your mind to expect to enjoy the reading.

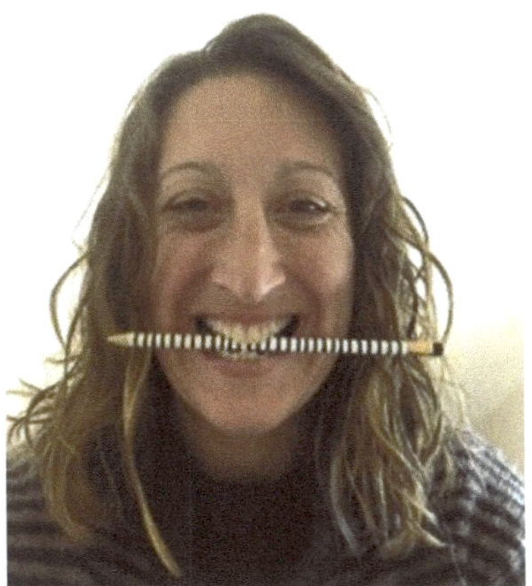

3. **Handwrite Notes**: Take out a pen and notebook and take notes about your thinking and learning by hand. Handwriting notes is often more effective than typing them.

Notice how these three experiences impact you.

Our brains do not exist in a vacuum. The places we learn in and the characteristics of those places make a marked difference in our ability to learn. In this chapter we'll take a look at why and how the learning environment shapes students' experiences. This includes the physical tools and resources, the organization of materials, and the tone the space creates. Characteristics of the environment, such as the type and level of noise, impact students' learning. For each research finding I'll share practical and often small tweaks you can make in your classroom space to support student success. This section will help you understand the following:

- The role nature awareness plays in learning
- The ways sound and music can impact students as they read
- How handwriting positively impacts learning
- Why reading print books leads to higher levels of comprehension
- Which materials you'll want to have available in your classroom space

All of us are learning in spaces that have a direct impact on our focus, attention, and ability to do deep learning. Each classroom has a set of affordances that shape our bodily experience in that space. Krueger (2024) explains,

> Affordances are action-possibilities, ways of relating to and acting on our world and things in it. From the moment we wake up in the morning, we're constantly doing things. We open our eyes and reach for our phone to check our email or scroll through social media. Eventually, we get up, make coffee, shower, get dressed, walk the dog, talk to people. . . . As we do these things, we continually rely on the resources and interactive possibilities that things, spaces, and other people furnish. To move through the world is to move through a rich landscape of affordances. (p. 3)

These affordances can intentionally be curated to support all of the students in your classroom. Some examples of affordances in literacy classrooms include the following:

- Charts
- Furniture: tables, desks, chairs
- Bookcases and books
- Notebooks and pens
- E-readers
- Laptops and other devices
- Windows
- Lighting
- Sticky notes
- Pointers and trackers
- Noise-canceling headphones

Affordances provide the possibility of students using them to take specific actions. For example, a sticky note provides the opportunity for a student to mark a place and also then revisit it. Without the sticky note, that action might not be possible.

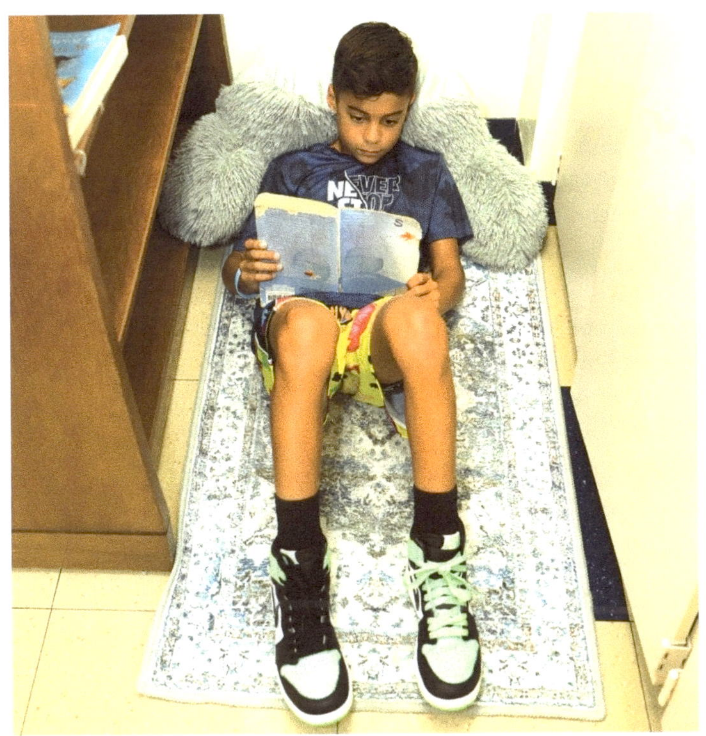

As teachers who have a variety of types of thinkers in our classroom, we can look at the affordances we've made available and ask what else might help students be successful. Sometimes the absence or presence of something in the classroom is the difference between engaged and active learners and those who struggle to focus and finish.

HOW DOES NATURE HELP STUDENTS?

Some of us teach in schools with picturesque views out of windows, playgrounds surrounded by trees, and quads with gardens. Others of us teach in buildings that are surrounded by concrete, next to highways, and have no windows at all. Despite this difference, all of us benefit from time spent in nature or viewing nature, even if just for one minute. Time spent in nature has shown to support students in so many ways. People who spend time in nature experience

- less stress and rumination and more awe,
- more focus and less impulsivity,
- an increase in working memory,
- increased creativity,
- more cooperation with others, and
- higher math and English language arts test scores. (Paul, 2021)

The good news is that if you don't have direct access to nature in your classroom, there are simulated ways to get the benefits.

Less Stress and More Awe

Researcher Kalevi Mikael Korpela coined the term *environmental self-regulation* to describe a process of psychological renewal that our brains cannot do on their own. In fact, researchers have demonstrated that what we think of as preferences for the types of settings we inhabit are our human survival instincts. People tend to prefer places that look safe and are resource rich, that allow us to see for many miles in all directions, and have some mystery to them (Fischer & Shrout, 2006). We now know that these preferences for spending time in natural places offer powerful ways to calm stress and maintain our equilibrium. Researchers have found that "the more stressed individuals are, the more benefit they derive from exposure to nature" (Paul, 2021, p. 95).

In order to measure the effects of time spent in nature on negative thinking and rumination, researchers asked participants to go for a ninety-minute walk. Half the participants walked in a quiet, leafy natural area while the other half walked next to a busy, loud roadway. Both brain scans and self-reports showed that people who spent time in the quiet nature landscape had less rumination and fewer negative thinking patterns (Jiang et al., 2014). The cycling through of negative thoughts is a common characteristic of those who suffer from depression. By getting a reprieve from rumination, individuals reserve more of their mental resources, which can be used for learning. Students who are stuck in rumination may have less bandwidth to recall information because they are using their energy in other ways.

A different set of studies found that people who spend time in nature experience more awe (Joye et al., 2015). Awe is the feeling of reverence, admiration, and heightened awareness. It shifts our perspectives. I think of the first time I climbed a tall mountain summit on a hike and witnessed my hometown from high above. Or the time my son flew on a plane and stared down in amazement at the clouds. Awe might also be the feeling you have when watching the sunset, a bee pollinate a flower, or waves crashing on a beach.

There are physical moves that accompany awe. We stop, pause, stare with wide open eyes, and our features slack (Shiota et al., 2003). The physicality prompts psychological shifts. Researchers found that awe helps us become more curious, more open-minded, and more willing to revise our previous thinking. Awe can be described as a "reset button for the human brain" (Haidt, 2012). Scientists found that when we experience awe, the boundary between ourselves and others starts to blur and we feel more connected to other people (Zelenski et al., 2015). Participants who viewed nature scenery videos were more likely to share and cooperate with others. This finding is interpreted as humans' ability to let go of individual interests and tap into the collective interests we all share by experiencing awe together.

While less time spent ruminating and more time spent in awe may seem far removed from students reading, thinking, and discussing in class, there are real connections. Recall from Chapter 3 how important a sense of safety and regulation is for students to actually focus on learning. If students are in environments where they spend a lot of time playing negative thoughts over and over again in their minds they cannot possibly have enough mental energy to participate in a close reading or class discussion with text evidence. Even the youngest students may enter the classroom stuck in ruminations about all that could go wrong. How will they focus on identifying rhymes or digraphs if they are replaying negative scenarios in their mind? When students can quiet the negative thought patterns, even a bit, they create space to notice. That noticing may lead to awe, which may lead to more creative and cooperative classroom experiences.

Many teachers have seen firsthand how reading nonfiction, especially nonfiction with vivid images, creates moments of awe for students. Reading nonfiction may include reading videos, photographs, infographics, as well as books. The first time a group of sixth graders I was teaching read a video of an underwater camera filming a single-celled organism called a *Xenophyophorea*, they showed the physical signs of awe. Their eyes opened wide, their mouths dropped, and they sat in silence. They seemed mesmerized by the tiny living creatures and the opportunity to witness them up close in the darkest depths of the ocean via video. After viewing this video, they read articles about the organism and then discussed their learning. The level of engagement happened only because the moments of awe captured them so raptly that they couldn't help but share their thinking with one another. Choosing texts and topics that may inspire awe is one way to engage students both physically and psychologically as readers.

Paying Attention

Voluntary attention is our directed attention. It is what we tend to think of when we ask someone to "please pay attention." Of course, students are always paying attention, but it might not be focused on what we would like them to do. We ask students to use voluntary or directed attention all day long in school—when reading, participating in a conversation, or listening to our lesson. The tricky thing about voluntary attention is that students get exhausted and often cannot sustain it for long periods of time.

Involuntary attention is when we spontaneously allow our environment to grab our attention. This might mean noticing the shape of clouds, hearing a birdsong, or watching the wind blow the leaves on a tree. Being in nature encourages involuntary attention and gives our voluntary attention a break (Kuo et al., 2018). The key aspect of involuntary attention is that we don't direct it. We cannot tell our students to go notice three things in nature. That would be another example of voluntary attention. Instead, we'd just offer time for students to observe nature, even from out of the window, in more of an open-ended way. Each person's body would notice on its own by simply bringing awareness to the natural space. This form of attention would give a much needed break to students so they would be better able to use more voluntary attention later in class.

Some programs call these "brain breaks," but in reality the brain is never taking a break; instead, it is given space to use involuntary attention. Researchers who study involuntary attention claim there are two important features to setting ourselves up for involuntary attention in nature. One includes "open monitoring," which means we bring curiosity and a nonjudgmental lens to the experience (Lymeus et al., 2020). The second is called "soft gazing," which comes from the practice of tai chi and is a mindfulness approach to receiving what is there to be seen (Morgan & Abrahamson, 2018). In many ways, students enter school already proficient in these two features and all of the time spent on voluntary attention in school means they may just need more time and space to remember what it feels like to be in the moment without a tangible goal in mind.

Researchers found that classroom engagement and time on task were higher in the outdoor learning environment than indoor classrooms (Kuo et al., 2018). They also looked at what happened back inside the classroom after the teachers had taken the class outside for a lesson. They did this based on teachers' concerns that students would have trouble getting back on task when coming back inside the classroom. Students who were taught outside in nature were actually more focused and more engaged both during and after the outdoor lessons. They found that teachers only had to redirect students every 6.5 minutes in the group who had outdoor learning compared to 3.5 minutes with the group who had indoor learning only. This may help those of us teachers who are concerned about student behaviors during and after lessons outside, as research has shown only positive impacts on student engagement. The researchers explain that "lessons in nature boost subsequent classroom engagement, and boost it a great deal; after a lesson in nature, teachers were able to teach for almost twice as long without having to interrupt instruction to redirect students' attention. This nature advantage persisted across 10 different weeks and lesson topics" (Kuo et al., 2018).

In one study, viewing images of nature led to less impulsivity and more self-control. Participants were shown photos of either natural settings like forests and mountains or urban settings such as buildings and roads. The study found that even images of

nature have positive effects. The participants who viewed the natural environment photos were more likely to postpone gratification, be less impulsive, and have more self-control than those who looked at urban photographs (Berry et al., 2015). Another study found that people who experienced images of nature were ten to sixteen percent more likely to restrain impulses than those who experienced a city landscape (van der Wal et al., 2013). Part of the interpretation of these findings is the belief that "when we see or experience an urban setting we are primed to be competitive, to believe we need to grab what's available. Nature, by contrast, inspires a feeling of abundance, a reassuring sense of permanence" (Paul, 2021, p. 108).

To be clear, I have lived much of my adult life in cities (Boston and New York City). I love cities and work collaboratively with many teachers and students who live and work in urban settings. This is not a judgment about these places. There is so much that cities offer in terms of culture, art, food, and convenience, to name just a few. This research is meant to show that even in thriving cities, a bit of nature awareness can really help us and our students. "We don't need to wait for the perfect weather, or to find our way to some unspoiled wilderness; any form of nature, under any conditions will do" (Paul, 2021, p. 97).

Working Memory

Time spent in nature or viewing nature also leads to gains in working memory (Bratman et al., 2015). Working memory is the ability to hold on to information and use it right away for the given task. "When we talk of working memory, we often include not only the memory itself, but also the executive control skills that are used to manage information in working memory and the cognitive processing of information" (Cowan, 2014). Many students struggle with reading longer texts because of working memory challenges. For example, a student may have to remember who each character is and keep them straight, hold on to the major plot points, recognize shifts in time and place (setting), and metacognitively track their thinking and ideas. All of these require a great deal of working memory. What may look like a misunderstanding or comprehension issue may really be a working memory challenge.

Researchers from the Landscape and Human Health Lab found that natural surroundings are tied to enhanced working memory. This means they found that students showed increases in concentration and self-control from spending time in nature. They also found that people with views of nature score higher on tests of working memory, even when they did not go outside into it. In fact, even looking at a patch of nature from indoors can boost memory and attention. In one specific study they found that spending ten minutes looking at pictures of Nova Scotia scenery improved people's concentration (Kaplan & Berman, 2010).

The following list offers free and fairly easy ways to ease stress and rumination, encourage awe, boost attention, and improve working memory through more nature awareness.

NATURE-BASED SUPPORTS

- Help students find places with a view of nature to read and write.
- If your classroom view does not have a nature view, you can project a nature view on the wall or students can pull them up on their devices for a digital view.
- Include some nature scenery photos in slides when teaching to give students a voluntary attention break.
- If you do have access to nature on your campus, give breaks for walks or sitting in nature before reading or writing periods.
- Consider teaching some lessons outside.
- When students are asked to read and write at home, they can also benefit from finding a natural view or an outdoor space. Encourage students to set up a natural scenery homework space.

A LOOK IN THE MIRROR

Many of us adults may also notice how voluntary attention can be difficult to sustain. If you have ever sat through an end-of-the-day faculty meeting or an after-school professional learning community (PLC) meeting you likely know firsthand that at a certain point you can no longer sustain direct attention. Some of the same tips for students also work for us teachers.

While I know your days are full and busy, taking a few minutes a day for nature awareness can really boost your own attention and working memory too. Consider trying the following:

- Sit outside on a lunch break or prep.
- Go for a short walk without focused attention. Just let your body and mind notice your surroundings.
- Encourage your grade level or PLC to meet outside (weather permitting).
- Create a digital natural scene and project it during transitions between periods.
- If possible, open windows if you are in an area where you can hear birds.
- Purposefully look out the window to give yourself a voluntary attention break.

HOW DOES LISTENING TO MUSIC IMPACT STUDENTS AS THEY READ?

Many students claim that listening to music helps them focus as they read, and it is not uncommon to see secondary students wearing earbuds during reading experiences. Research does not necessarily support this claim. There is some nuance here and it is not as simple as suggesting there should never be music or background noise. In my own experience as an adult reader, I would say background noise sometimes helps, sometimes distracts, and sometimes has little to no impact at all on me. Let's see what the research says.

One study conducted with seventh and eighth graders looked at the impact listening to pop music while reading had on students' comprehension (Anderson & Fuller, 2010). Over three hundred students were split into two groups. One group did not listen to music while another group listened to Billboard top hits as they read. Students were then given standardized and norm referenced reading tests to measure comprehension. Listening to music had a negative effect on reading comprehension. Students were then asked to self-report whether they had a preference for listening to music as they read. This detrimental effect on reading comprehension was also seen in those students who had a preference for listening to music. Based on this study, it would seem students should be advised not to listen to music as they read. It is important to note that this study looked at the impact of lyrical music. Other studies were designed to look at background music and sounds in different ways.

Mood and Arousal

A series of studies found that listening to some kinds of music had an overall positive effect on students' learning outcomes. This was based on the arousal-mood hypothesis that claims that students need to have the right amount of physical arousal in order to maintain attention and focus on the learning task. Some researchers claim that a piece of music needs to be in the right tempo and mode to create the appropriate arousal and mood in the learner (Lehmann & Seufert, 2017). Yerkes and Dodson (1908) found that there is an optimal amount of arousal for learners that follows an inverted U-shape. Too much arousal makes students feel anxious and get distracted. Too little arousal means students are not engaged and invested in the learning process. A medium level of arousal is ideal for learning. Finding the right music to listen to can help some students get into that medium level of arousal. This may be why some students prefer listening to music as they read, to create enough arousal that they can engage with the text.

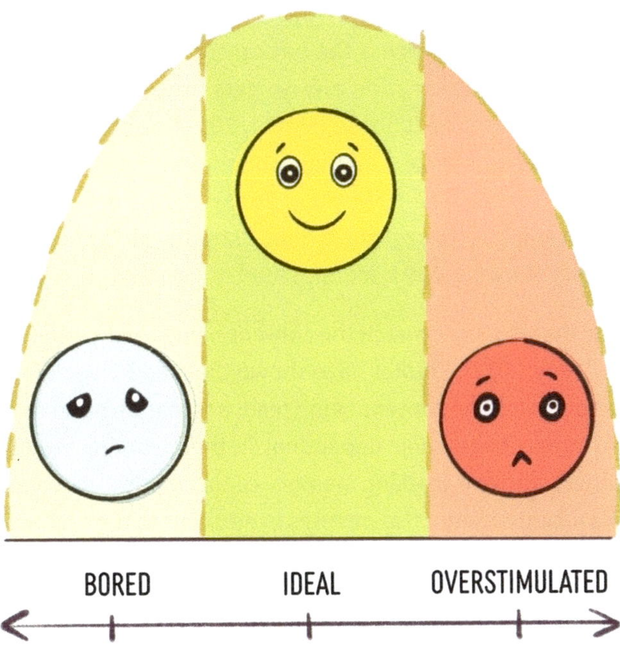

Self-Reflection on Mood: Use the inverted-U visual to explain to students why listening to music may not be helping them.

A multi-study analysis conducted by Lehmann and Seufert (2017) drew the following conclusions on the effects of background music on learners.

- Background music influences mood. (Juslin & O'Neill, 2001; Juslin & Sloboda, 2001; Schmidt & Trainor, 2010)
- Background music leads to different emotions (depending on major or minor key). (Husain et al., 2002)
- Mood influences learning. (Goetz & Hall, 2013; Heuer & Reisberg, 2014; Pekrun, 2006; Pekrun et al., 2017)
- Positive mood is associated with better learning outcomes. (Isen, 2002)
- Negative mood or boredom hinders learning. (Pekrun, 2006)

Based on these studies, we could decide that listening to the right music would prime students into being in the right mood and that it would help them as they read.

Cognitive Load

A different set of studies about background music looks at how the brain shifts between paying attention to the music versus the text being read. In these studies, researchers claim that the learner has to divide their attention between two tasks, which is potentially taking away from reading. Students "have to invest cognitive resources to process the background music in addition to the learning task, as auditive information always gets processed first (Salamé & Baddeley, 1989) and cannot be ignored (Mayer, 2001)" (Lehmann & Seufert, 2017). Researchers who study cognitive load have concluded that listening to music has a negative effect on learners (Kämpfe et al., 2011). Diving deeper, claims have been made that listening to background music creates an "unnecessary burden" on working memory (Cowan, 2001; Miller, 1994).

Listening to music that does not match the content being read is referred to as a "seductive detail" (Rey, 2012). Studies have shown that seductive details, such as pictures that do not match the content being read, and background music have different kinds of impact on learners depending on their working memory capacity. In one study learners with low working memory capacity performed worse when the reading materials included seductive pictures in addition to the text. But learners with higher working memory capacity were not negatively affected by seductive pictures (Sanchez & Wiley, 2006). Researchers claimed that this seductive detail impact transfers to background music as well. This means that depending on the students' working memory, background music may have a negative impact or no impact at all. Lehmann and Seufert (2017) claim that "background music should only be considered when the learning material itself is not too demanding."

A study of students who were divided into four groups to compare the impact of music on their ability to revise revealed a clear negative impact on performance (Perham & Currie, 2014). Findings included the following:

- Students who revised in quiet environments performed over sixty percent better than those who revised listening to music that had lyrics.
- Students who listened to music without lyrics did better than those who had listened to music with lyrics.
- It made no difference if students revised listening to songs they liked or didn't like.

Based on the mixed results across different kinds of studies, the following guidelines could be helpful to share with students and consider when designing the norms of your classroom community.

- Listen to music before reading to prime yourself. Get yourself motivated and ready to learn.
- Avoid listening to music with lyrics while reading.
- If you struggle with working memory, then avoid music altogether when reading.
- Try to create quiet environments so all students can focus as they read.

WHY SHOULD STUDENTS HANDWRITE?

Since tech companies pushed schools to create a one-to-one device policy, investing millions of dollars into tablets and similar devices, and the rise of virtual school during the Covid-19 global pandemic, teachers and parents have noticed that students spend very little time actually writing by hand anymore. Debates about whether we should still teach cursive, how much screen time and what types are effective, as well as at what age students should shift to typing abound. There have been several studies that looked at the impact of note-taking by hand or by digital device and while there is a lot of nuance, most studies show the importance of learners spending more time writing by hand. There are also many benefits for the youngest learners to spend time handwriting letters as it sets them up for stronger foundational skills and leads to more brain connectivity.

Sensorimotor Input and Brain Connectivity

Learning the basics of early literacy, such as the ability to identify letters and then form the shapes that correspond to the letters, is tied to students' sensorimotor system. It is not just children's brains but also their sensorimotor movements that help them learn these vital foundational skills.

The way young children learn about objects is tied to their perceptions of the objects and the object's properties. In order to create a unified understanding of an object, children need to see it, touch it, move it, feel the texture, identify the size and shape, and experience a number of the object's properties. These experiences form a neural network. Eventually the entire network can be accessed when only one input is present (Martin et al., 2000; Pulvermüller, 1999).

If we think of letters as objects, this means students would benefit from time looking at the letters; tracing letters; forming letters in the air, in sand, and with paper and pencil; and manipulating visual representations, such as magnetic letters and letter tiles. After these experiences, which allow students to build the neural network by combining visual and sensorimotor information, they can later simply see a letter and recognize it. This is one of the main reasons why handwriting letters is so important for young children.

In addition, because young children's first attempts at writing letters are often messy, they have to practice each letter often. The different versions of their emerging letter formation solidifies their recognition of the letters. The variability of ways to form a letter seems to help readers recognize it more than when they are viewing typed and uniform versions of the letters (James, 2017; J. X. Li & James, 2016). For example, when my son first learned to write his name, Leo, he used an uppercase E and wrote it with four horizontal lines instead of three. Over time this approximation went away and he now finds it funny that he ever wrote an E that way, but it was the messy, varied practice and perception of his own writing that helped him learn the letter. This variability also applies to cursive writing. Research has shown it is the handwriting, whether in cursive or print, that has benefits for students (Ose Askvik et al., 2020).

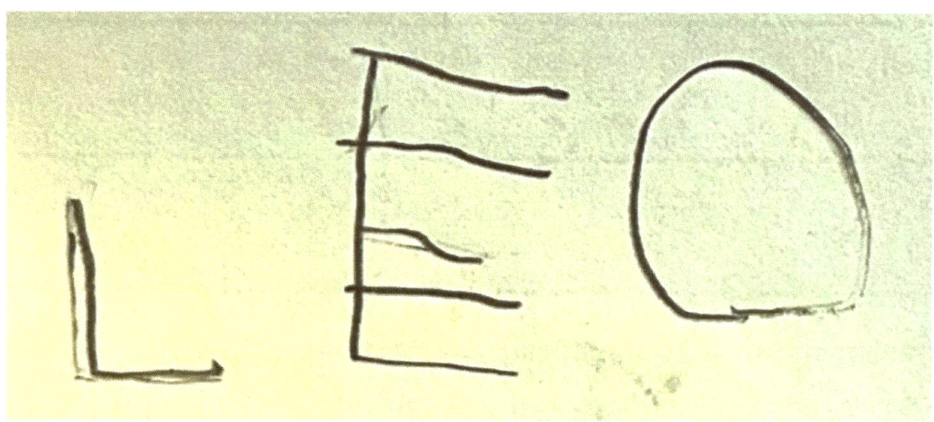

Several studies suggest there are sensorimotor benefits of handwriting letters.

- Handwriting has been shown to facilitate letter recognition and understanding in young readers (J. X. Li & James, 2016; Longcamp et al., 2005).
- When first graders handwrite words, it leads to better spelling (Cunningham & Stanovich, 1990). This was compared to typing or moving letter tiles to spell.
- Preschool students who practiced handwriting letters performed better in both letter and word writing than those who learned through typing (Kiefer et al., 2015).
- Handwriting leads to better memory and recall (Longcamp et al., 2006; Mueller & Oppenheimer, 2014; Smoker et al., 2009).
- In studies of students with pure alexia, which means they were no longer able to recognize letters visually, they were asked to trace the outline of letters with their fingers. This led to greater letter recognition (Bartolomeo et al., 2002; Seki et al., 1995).

A recent study of students' brains as they handwrite compared to when they type found a brain connectivity benefit that comes from handwriting. Since handwriting requires fine motor control over the fingers, it helps students to pay attention to what they are doing and to stay focused. When typing, the same repetitive movement of pushing down on a key is required. The lack of variance between pushing down on the letter T and the letter B means there is no sensorimotor difference between the two movements even though the letters themselves, if they were handwritten, would require very different fine motor control. "Whenever handwriting movements are included as a learning strategy, more of the brain gets stimulated, resulting in the formation of more complex neural network connectivity" (Van der Weel & Van der Meer, 2024).

The researchers only found increased brain connectivity when participants were writing by hand and not when they were pressing down on the keyboard. They also noticed that the connections between brain regions were linked to specific sensorimotor processes that are typical in handwriting. They claim that their study provides evidence that handwriting promotes learning (Van der Weel & Van der Meer, 2024).

Researchers also sought to understand whether digital pencils and tablet handwriting had the same effect as pencil-and-paper handwriting. During one seven-week study, preschool students were divided into three groups. One group was taught to write with pencil and paper, a second group was taught using a stylus and tablet, and a third group used a keyboard to type. The group using a pencil and paper, but not the group using the stylus and tablet, performed better on letter recognition. The paper-and-pencil group also showed improved visuospatial skills compared with the group using a virtual keyboard (Mayer, 2021). An interpretation of this finding is that the feedback that students get from the friction on the paper leads to greater sensorimotor processing than the tablet's smooth surface.

While the research supports handwriting with paper and pencil as it is more beneficial than using digital tools, special educators can also be reminded that some students need modifications based on varying abilities. For students who can hold a paper and pencil, the research supports teaching handwriting before introducing other digital tools.

TEACHING LETTER FORMATION TO YOUNG STUDENTS

- Invest in a research-based handwriting program that can consistently be used across grades.
- Use sensory experiences for letter formation practice.
  - Sand
  - Soap
  - Shaving cream
  - Sandpaper
  - Bumpy board

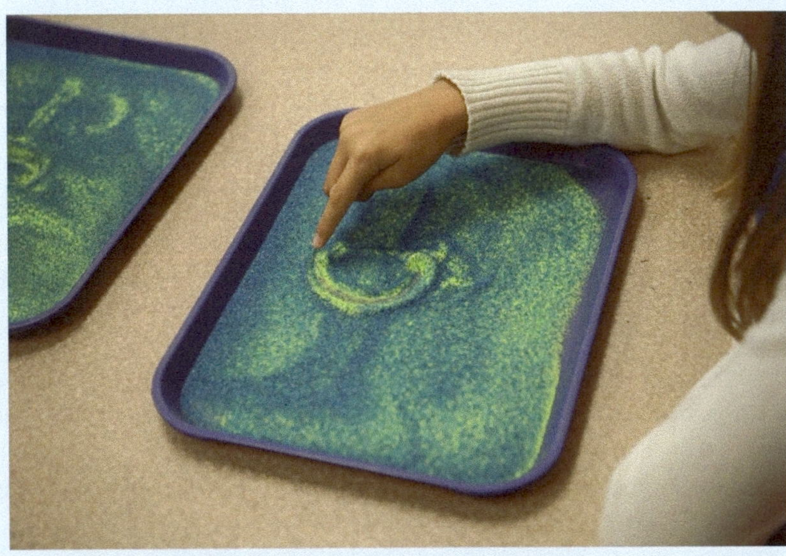

- Prompt students to move their bodies like the letters.
  - Write in the air
  - Make their body into the shape of the letter
- Use adjectives to describe the characteristics of the letters.
  - Long
  - Short
  - Curly
  - Straight, etc.
- Use the gradual release of responsibility when teaching letter formation.
  - Model: I go.
  - Guided practice: We go.
  - Independent practice: You go.

Conceptual Understanding

Moving beyond foundational skills with young students, we can look at the impact of handwriting on older students. Studies of college students who took notes by hand showed they performed better on tests of conceptual understanding than their peers who took notes on a laptop (Mueller & Oppenheimer, 2014). One of the conclusions of the studies is that students who took notes on the laptop tended to transcribe words verbatim rather than taking time to understand what was being said and make choices about what was worth writing down. Taking the time to make these sorts of choices about what to write and how to write it matters. Those who handwrote their notes were already processing information as they wrote. By putting things in their own words, they had to make sure they understood the concepts first.

Another aspect of handwriting notes that we can learn from is the importance of slowing down in order to be able to think. Typing verbatim (or copying and pasting notes from digital readings) is a fast process. A student could literally type up notes without understanding what they typed.

A second study, done in 2021, attempted to replicate the original study of laptop notes compared to handwriting (Urry et al., 2021). These researchers did not come to the same conclusions as those of the original study. Instead, they found that scores on a quiz taken directly after listening to a lecture were positively correlated with the amount of words the note-taker wrote down (the more the better) and whether the notes were in their own words or not. In this study they found it was not the device that had the impact but the note-takers' ability to put things in their own original words that helped them do better on the quiz.

Since notes are most effective when the learner has time to process and grasp concepts by writing about them in their own words, it would be most helpful to take some class time to teach this skill. There are at least four parts of note-taking so that conceptual understanding develops that can explicitly be taught to students.

1. Notice when something is important enough to write down.
2. Think about what the information means in the context of the reading.
3. Decide how the information fits with what you already know.
4. Write notes in a way that helps you organize the information.

While some students can do this level of thinking and note-taking on a device, there are many students who will take the shortcut and simply copy and paste or type verbatim. This is because they have so much practice with the more fluent, fast-paced, and frankly, easier note-taking method. I recommend giving students some experiences with sticky notes in the primary grades and notebooks in the secondary grades while you teach them how to take notes by hand in ways that support conceptual understanding. At first, older students may resist having to handwrite, but after they get more comfortable and get more practice. they tend to see the benefits. Almost all of my college-level students choose to take notes in class by hand. When I asked them why, they said it helps them learn more.

The following charts can be used to help students with the skill of note-taking, to reinforce conceptual understanding in developmentally appropriate ways (Appendix U).

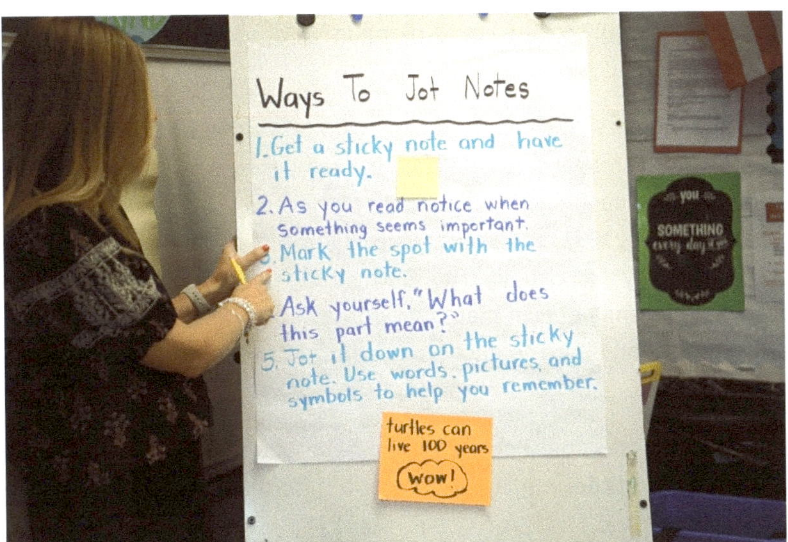

Ways to Take Notes

1. Get out a notebook and pen.
2. Remind yourself what the focus of the reading is. Jot the focus on the top of the page.
3. As you read, notice when a part of the text matches your focus for reading.
4. Ask yourself, "What does this mean?
5. Think about HOW this information fits with the larger topic/focus.
6. Jot down the page number and use your own words to capture what it says, what it means, and how it connects. Use words, sketches, tables, shapes, or symbols to help you remember your thinking.

A recent meta-analysis of note-taking at the college level also reinforced the idea that handwriting notes leads to better grades and a boost in memory (Flanigan et al., 2024). The authors of the study claim that it is the reviewing of notes that leads to higher achievement. They interpret their conclusions based on the fact that students who handwrite have to decide on what is important as they encounter the material, so they are thinking more about the information and staying more focused.

Another key element is that college students who take notes on a laptop tend not to capture any of the images from the class in their notes, while those who choose to handwrite do include images. The authors of the study claim, that dual-coding theory (Clark & Paivio, 1991) shows that learning occurs best when information is coded both verbally and visually. This is why it is helpful to model and support students in handwriting notes in their own words and to include visuals. Most importantly, they need time and encouragement to review those notes so they are actually being used.

The following self-assessment checklist can help students review their own notes to identify what they currently include and to make a plan for what they might try next.

Note-Taking Reflection Tool

Do my notes include . . .

- An organizational structure
- Visuals
- Key terms
- Ideas in my own words
- Important details
- Connections

Having a class routine is incredibly important for helping students develop the habit in class to take and use notes so that as they become future college students they already have this process down. For example, I often create a routine like this:

Note-Taking Habits

Before Reading	Take out your notebook and reread the entries from the past few days. Remind yourself what you have been reading about and thinking about.
While Reading	Decide on what to write down and how to write it. Don't just write down what the text says, but also write what you think about it (connections, questions, ideas, patterns, themes, etc.).
After Reading	Reread what you wrote and leave yourself a note about where you left off in your thinking so you can pick right back up tomorrow.
Before Conversation	Reread what you have been writing down, and choose a few ideas to talk about. Circle, star, or highlight possible conversation ideas.
During Conversation	When you get more evidence for your own idea, add it to your notes. When you hear a new idea you connect with, jot it down. When you hear an idea that pushes your thinking and makes you change your mind, add that to your notes.
After Conversation	Take a minute to summarize the big takeaways from the conversation in your notes. You can also jot down further questions you want to keep thinking about.

For younger students, you can create a similar routine, but do it with your students instead of expecting them to do the note-taking on their own. For example, in a whole class read-aloud you can write down what students say on class chart paper or large sticky notes. This models the routines they will later do on their own.

A LOOK IN THE MIRROR

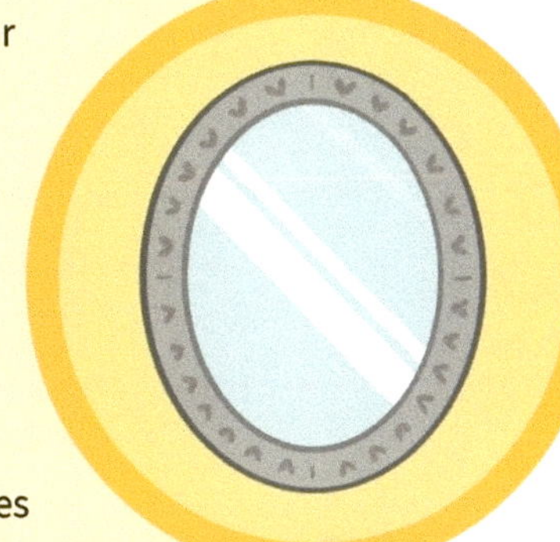

Handwriting notes can be helpful for us adults too. Researchers found that something called the ownership effect impacts our ability to read our own handwriting compared to reading someone else's (Vinci-Boohr et al., 2019). Ownership effect is described as the phenomenon where we find something to have more value and be more attractive because we view it as belonging to us. This means that when we take our own notes and then review them, we not only get the handwriting benefits of developing more conceptual understanding and memory, but we also tend to find the notes more useful because we created them.

If you see the benefit of handwriting but also lack the organization to find that sheet of paper or notebook, consider a digital notebook. A Rocketbook allows you to easily snap a photo of the notes with their app, and they are automatically scanned and organized into folders for you. You can decide who to share them with and even link them to other documents or reminders.

WHY SHOULD STUDENTS READ PRINT TEXTS?

Several researchers and writers have documented the ways that digital reading is different from reading print texts. Of note is Wolf's (2018) bestselling book, *Reader, Come Home,* in which the cognitive scientist argues that the digital world is impacting students' ability to focus, read with depth, and participate in critical thinking. She warns us of the negative effects of skimming and just getting the gist of a text.

Other researchers conducted studies that compared e-readers and print books. Findings reveal a mixture of results (not unlike the research on handwriting notes) that remind us there is nuance we need to keep in mind. A few key findings to note include the following:

- Comprehension is six to eight times better with physical books than e-readers (Altamura et al., 2023).
- Students with high reading comprehension skills show similar levels of comprehension when reading on tablets as they do when reading a print

text, even under time pressure. Students with lower comprehension skills had difficulties comprehending digital texts while under time pressure (Cho et al., 2021).

- In elementary and middle school there is a negative relationship observed between leisure digital reading and text comprehension, while at the high school and university level the relationship turns positive (Altamura et al., 2023).
- Ninety-two percent of students reported that they prefer reading print books over e-books (Baron, 2015).
- Some students with dyslexia benefit from the modification of seeing fewer words on the screen that e-readers provide (Schneps et al., 2013).
- Looking back into a paper text leads to greater comprehension. Readers of digital texts tend not to look back in the text (Goodwin et al., 2020).

Sensorimotor Impact

Since entire books have been written and will continue to be written on digital reading, I will focus only on the sensorimotor implications of print reading for students. Similar to the research on writing by hand, there is a sensorimotor component to reading that is different when students read on electronic devices versus print books. Just like the act of pressing down on the keys while typing uses the same movement for all letters, reading a digital book has the same physical movement whether you are reading a two hundred page novel or a twenty-five page picture book. But, when you hold a print novel in your hands you can visually see the width, you get physical feedback when you turn the page, and you are oriented to the location of where information is within the context of the text. These sensorimotor experiences are really important when it comes to aspects of reading comprehension.

Let's look at a few of the differences in movement experiences, or affordances, between print texts and digital texts.

Print Texts	Digital Texts
• Each text has a unique feel to it • Feel the book's weight • See the size of the book's perimeter • Feel differences in paper quality • See the width of the spine • Physically turn a page • See where in the text a detail is located • Can highlight and write directly into the text • Can flip back to a page with ease and mark it with a sticky note or fold down the corner of the page	• All texts feel the same • All texts weigh the same • All texts have the same size • The texture is consistent • Unclear how long the book is visually • Click or slide across the screen to get to the next "page" • No visual map of where the details are located • May be able to use tools depending on the device, e.g., slide a finger to highlight and/or type a note • May be able to locate previous pages if you bookmarked them and if the device has that feature

Cognitive Map

In a similar way to how people construct a mental map of a place (e.g., noting where the doors, stairs, and bathroom are), readers create a cognitive map of the physical location of a text and its spatial relationship to the page as a whole (Jabr, 2013; L.-Y. Li et al., 2013; Payne & Reader, 2006). For example, when reading an article in print form, I know the table was on the left side about four pages in. This is tied to the concept of spatial awareness. We may not think a lot about the role that spatial awareness plays in reading, but it does have an important role. Because holding a book in your hand and turning the pages has a specific sensorimotor component to it, there is an "index" in the brain that helps readers map what is read visually to a particular page (Rothkopf & Coatney, 1974).

On a digital device, the indexing of where to locate information is much harder to create. Reading on screens makes it difficult for students to construct an effective *cognitive map*, or spatial representation, of the text (L.-Y. Li et al., 2013; Payne & Reader, 2006). Hou et al. (2017) explain, "screens, in general, weaken the spatial cues about a reader's location in a text (Dillon, 1992; Liesaputra & Witten, 2012; McDonald & Stevenson, 1998; O'Hara & Sellen, 1997), and they impede the reader in forming an effective cognitive map (Jabr, 2013; L.-Y. Li et al., 2013)" (p. 85). When a student does not construct a cognitive map, they have to use greater cognitive resources to navigate texts and to retain information. This means the student has less capacity for information recall and comprehension (L.-Y. Li et al., 2013). This is tied to a student's ability to know where they are in the text so they don't get lost.

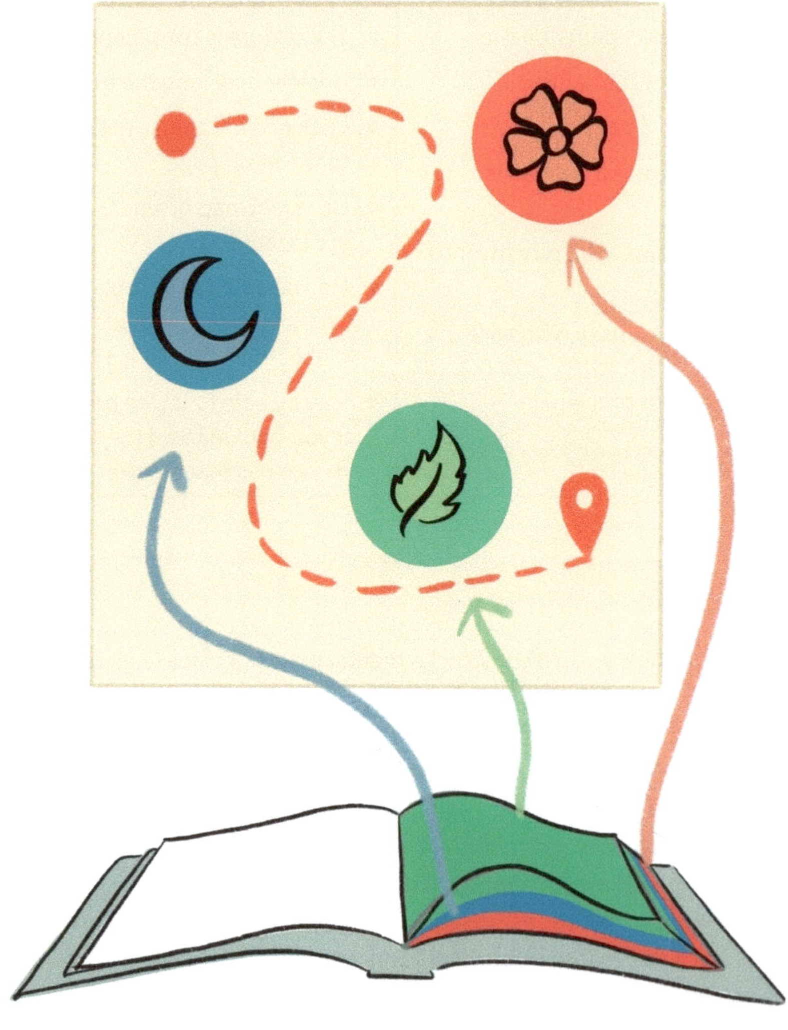

During a keynote address at the Learning and the Brain Conference (February 24, 2024), cognitive scientist Jared Cooney Horvath described the following elements that are connected to cognitive mapping and reading. First, memory is based on knowing location. In order to know the location we need stability, perception of depth, and a three-dimensional location map. In a reading example this means we would want the text to stay the same, for example, not changing the font size. It also means we need to know how far into the text any given information is located. We would know we are halfway through a book that is two inches wide along the spine. This helps us have a three-dimensional experience and makes the text an actual object we can map. He also went on to claim that standardized tests should not be digital because digital texts do not allow for this sort of location experience.

While we aren't in charge of selecting texts in standardized tests, we are able to make choices about digital and print texts in our own classrooms, at least some of the time. I know there are real barriers to getting print texts in students' hands in many schools. These barriers may include lack of funding for books, no copy paper or printers, and administrative mandates to use those expensive devices. For many students though, it is essential that they spend most of their time, at least while they are reading closely, holding print texts. The research in this section leads me to think that students' reading experience with anything new or complex should first happen in print text. As standardized testing draws closer, it does make sense for students to have instruction and practice reading on digital devices.

TIPS FOR READING DIGITAL TEXTS

Assume that when you switch to digital reading experiences, students will likely benefit from

- keeping the font size stable throughout the text,
- previewing the text as much as possible to predict text structure and attempt some indexing,
- having a paper and pen in hand to try to make a cognitive map as you read, and
- discussing with students how to stay focused and not just skim read when on a digital device.

WHICH MATERIALS SHOULD BE AVAILABLE IN THE CLASSROOM TO SUPPORT LEARNING?

This chapter began with a description about affordances—the possibility that objects bring for movement and learning in the classroom. The following table is a synthesis of the key ideas from across the book that are tied to objects you'll want to consider including in the classroom. While the exact materials in a first-grade classroom will often look different than in a ninth-grade classroom, I trust you will adapt this list and make it work for your particular students.

Classroom Materials (Appendix V)

Materials	Why They Are Helpful
Bins with handles	Organize materials so that students experience the flexion/pulling movement that can lead to more positive feelings
Charts for students	Support student reflection and application of strategies you taught
Earbuds/headphones/speakers	Listen to music before work to create motivation and arousal
Comprehension manipulatives (see page 128)	Allows and encourages students to incorporate movement into learning experiences in order to deepen understanding
Nature view (or slides)	Reduces stress and increases awe, leads to more focused attention and less impulsivity
Notebooks	Students can take notes by handwriting to develop conceptual understanding
Pens, pencils, highlighters	Students can take notes in the text and develop conceptual understanding
Print texts	Students can have the sensorimotor experience and develop spatial awareness by reading physical texts
Sensory materials (shave cream, sand, bumpy boards)	Practice handwriting and have sensorimotor experiences for foundational skills
Sticky notes	Mark and locate information and help with indexing and creating a cognitive map of a text
Sensory seating and wobble cushions that allow students to move while still sitting	Create opportunities for movement without having to get up and distract others and provide sensory feedback

A SUMMARY OF KEY IDEAS FROM CHAPTER 7

In this chapter we looked at the possibilities that learning spaces offer students. Classroom spaces have a direct impact on students' level of stress, ability to have focused attention, memory, mood, cognitive load, and conceptual understanding, all of which are connected to students' reading, writing, and thinking skills.

- Time in or viewing nature helps students experience less stress, pay more attention, and support working memory. Small moments of nature awareness can be woven into class time and help students increase focus and be less impulsive.
- Background sound most likely has a negative impact on students, even if they claim they prefer it. While students can get the benefit of mood and motivation boosts by listening to music before reading, many students will benefit from not listening to music while reading.
- Handwriting positively impacts young students by supporting their letter recognition, spelling, and memory. Handwriting notes support conceptual understanding in students of all ages.
- Reading print books has a specific sensorimotor experience that helps readers create cognitive maps and leads to deeper comprehension.
- By curating specific materials and manipulatives in your classroom space, you can set students up to be successful.

A SUMMARY OF PRACTICES FROM CHAPTER 7

Practice	Reflection Questions	When and Where I May Use This
Incorporate some nature-based supports into your classroom (page 178).	How might I help students get more time in nature? Which digital nature images do my students enjoy?	
Create time for students' self-reflection on their current physiological state (page 181).	How might I help students honestly self-reflect on their level of arousal? How might grounding experiences from Chapter 3 support this practice?	
Teach letter formation to young students using sensory experiences and materials (page 186).	Which sensory experiences would help my students with letter formation? How can I adapt letter formation practices for older students who could use some help with handwriting?	
Model ways to take notes by hand (page 189).	How might we use more consistent approaches to note-taking across content areas?	
Use the note-taking reflection tool with students so they can set goals (page 190).	How do students feel about their notes? What next steps can students identify that would help their note-taking effectiveness?	
Make note-taking routines lasting habits (page 191).	Which habits do I want to help students create? What reminders can I put in place to help make this consistent?	
Teach students tips for reading digital texts (page 197).	How can I help students see the differences in print-based and digital reading? What balance might I strike?	
Curate and collect classroom materials to support body and brain integration (page 199).	Which materials might I add to the classroom? How can I explain their use to students so they feel ownership of them too?	

Section

III

Designing Learning Experiences Based on the Body and Brain Connection

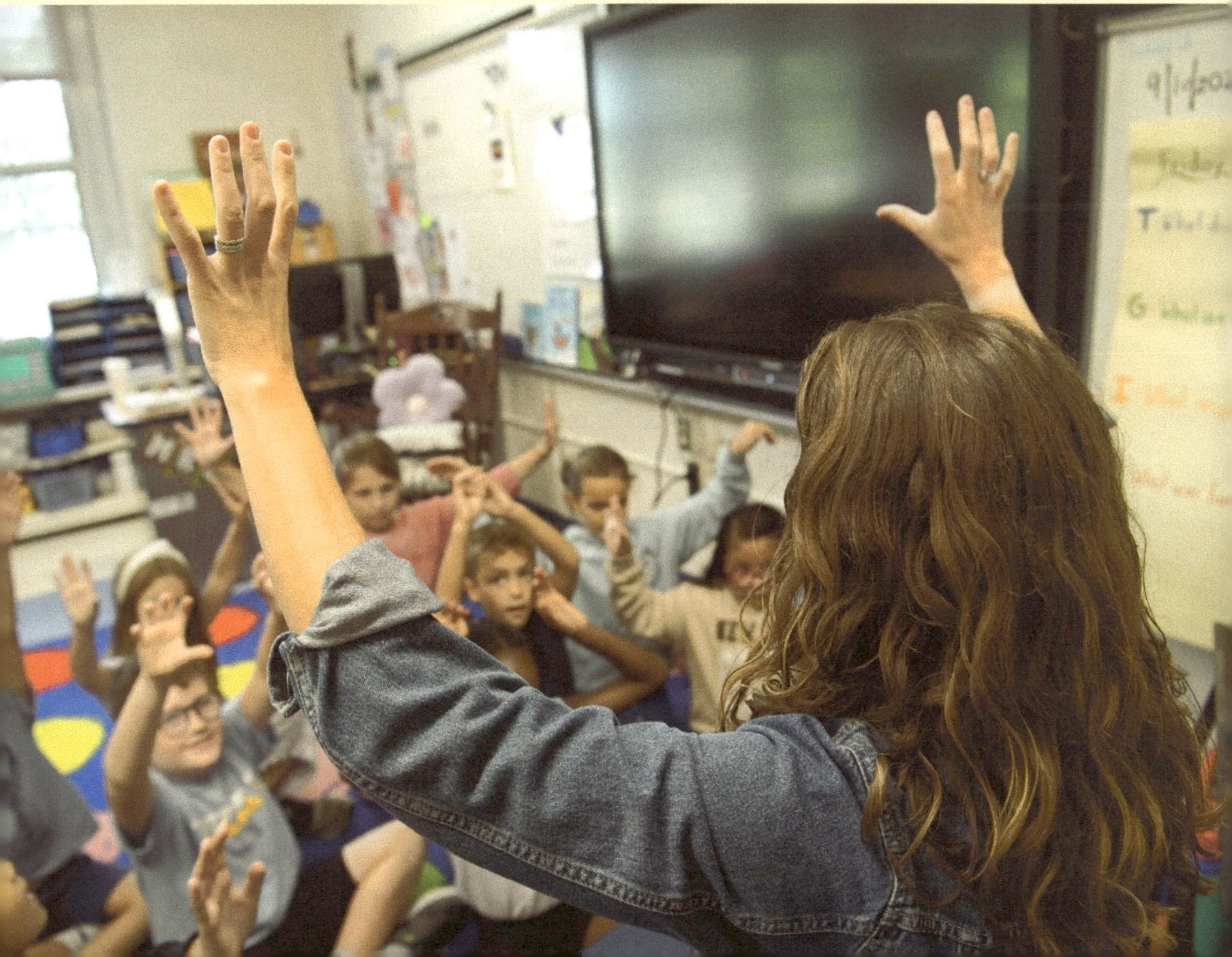

Chapter 8

Putting It All Together

"Most of us think of ourselves as thinking creatures that feel, but we are actually feeling creatures that think."

— Jill Bolte Taylor

I sat around a table with a few other educators, some working with elementary students and some with secondary, and I listened as they named the many challenges students presented. Every one of them was related to the students' bodies—whether it be the challenge itself or a possible solution. One student couldn't sit still and focus, another student seemed totally disengaged and distant, some students refused to talk in class, and others dominated the class leaving little space for others. As I listened, I was reminded of the incredible impact of our bodies and the toolkit of practices we could use to support all students if we considered more body and brain based strategies.

This team of educators stepped into classrooms with me. I taught several different classes across Grades 1 through 12, and I started every lesson with a grounding practice from this book. It didn't matter if the students were five or eighteen, every single classroom felt like a massive exhale, and we could see the difference in the level of focus in the room when we were done. As we moved into the content of the lesson, students (and I) were visibly ready to learn. When students began discussing their ideas with their partners, they moved their hands in gesture. Later when students began to read, they opened up notebooks, took out stickies, actively jotted down thinking, and made maps of their ideas. Every part of the learning experience was an example of the body and brain connection.

Step inside a classroom lesson focused on interpreting figurative language. As you watch, notice the practices you've read about from across the book. You'll see a grounding practice, intentional gestures, different types of movements, varied seating options, and the use of manipulatives.

WHAT DOES A BODY AND BRAIN CONNECTED ELEMENTARY LESSON LOOK LIKE?

The following lesson is one example to help you imagine how many of the practices described across this book can come together in an elementary school lesson. You can use this example to inspire your own. Please note that this lesson would only work after smaller steps are taken. The teacher cannot simply jump into this sort of lesson without teaching each part first. For example, first the teacher would teach the what and why of grounding experiences. Then they would set up routines for gathering, etc. The lesson that follows shows how it all can fit together, after the parts have all been taught and practiced.

Part of the Lesson	Example
Ground	Students were led through a calm breathing experience for the first minute of class.
Gather	The teacher asked students to gather on the carpet, sitting next to their partner, near the view of the park. Students had spots that worked for them, based on their individual physical needs. A few had fidget toys in their hands, two were sitting on wiggle seats, and some had spots in the back so they could stand up if they needed to without interrupting others.
Teach	The teacher modeled how to preview an informational article, using text features to predict what they would learn about. As the teacher modeled, they pointed to a chart of features and also used a gesture for each one. For example, for photographs the teacher made a click gesture like taking a photo, for maps they gestured opening up a map, and for headings they pointed to their head.
Make a Plan	After the modeling, students made plans with their partners. First, they used the class chart to summarize what they just learned. Many students began using the same gestures the teacher modeled. They clicked, opened hands, and pointed. Second, they talked to each other about which comprehension manipulatives they wanted to use to help them. They went back to their seats and took out what they needed from their small baggy of manipulatives.
Read/Write/ Think/Do	Students began previewing the texts. Some had sticky notes out and were using them to mark text features. A few gestured as they located them and used them. One pair of students used colored blocks that represented each feature. They had blue for maps, green for headings, etc. They put a colored block next to the text when they found one. For those not using manipulatives, they still used movement to point, lean in and look closer, and smile at cool-looking images. After the previewing, students were reminded to use the features they noticed to make a prediction. Students used what they knew about note-taking to write down their predictions. Some used a box, some used a web, and some made a quick sketch.

(Continued)

(Continued)

Part of the Lesson	Example
Share	Partners met up and shared what they predicted and which features helped them make the predictions. Many students were showing their notes and pointing, some were gesturing, and a few were even standing up and acting out.
Read/Write/ Think/Do	The teacher anticipated that students would need that sharing time before reading because their stamina tends to wane at this two-thirds point in the period. After the share, the students went back to reading on their own, using their predictions to guide what they thought about. Partners sat side-by-side as positive supports. As students read, they took notes and used stickies. Most were not sitting totally still, but they were focused and actively engaged.
Reflect	As the period came to an end, the teacher asked students to self-reflect, using the predictions they began with. Students were asked to think about whether their predictions were accurate or if they needed to revise them. Students thought, many pointing to a pretend thought bubble over their heads, and then they went back and either put a star next to their prediction if they still thought it or added or changed it if they had new thinking.

WHAT DOES A BODY AND BRAIN CONNECTED PERIOD LOOK LIKE IN A SECONDARY CLASSROOM?

The following lesson is one example to help you imagine how many of the practices described across this book can come together in a secondary classroom. You can use this example to inspire your own.

Part of the Lesson	Example
Ground	Students were led through an experience of visualizing personal power to get grounded and ready to learn.
Gather	The teacher asked students to huddle. As a class, students worked with the teacher to find their huddle spot. For some that was standing in a semi-circle, for some that meant sitting on a few wobble stools that were near the huddle area, and for some they stayed in a chair. They spent earlier in the year rehearsing this, so it was seamless and quick.
Teach	The teacher modeled how to synthesize ideas from across two texts the class was reading. The first was a video clip they read the day before and the other was an article they read earlier in the week. The teacher used their hands to act out what synthesis means by showing how each hand is a text and then clasped them together to show they can form one bigger idea. Then the teacher went through a process of showing how a smaller idea from text A and a smaller idea from text B can form a larger idea. She had sticky notes that were smaller with the smaller ideas jotted on them and then a larger, blank sticky note ready to model the bigger idea. Text A Storms are causing massive beach erosion. Text B "Once-in-a-lifetime" storms happen every year now More frequent, destructive storms are causing massive beach erosion, leading to higher expenses, more rebuilding of homes, and animal habitat displacement.

(Continued)

(Continued)

Part of the Lesson	Example
Make a Plan	After the modeling, students made plans with their partners. First, they used the examples on the stickies to summarize what they just learned. Many students began using the same gestures the teacher modeled, because they were prompted to. They took two hands and brought them together. Students had different text sets based on their own research topics they were studying. This means they made a plan for how they could apply what they had just learned to their own texts. They took out folders with previously read articles and notes and sorted through them until they found two that went together in some way.
Read/Write/ Think/Do	Students began working on their own to synthesize ideas across the two texts they identified. Many took out different sized stickies like the ones the teacher modeled with. Some drew boxes in their notebooks instead.
Share With Partners	Partners met up and shared the two smaller ideas and the larger synthesized idea with one another. Some pointed to notes, some gestured like the teacher modeled, and one group used Lego pieces of different sizes to represent the small and big ideas and then put the two small ideas together to form a bigger one.
Share With the Whole Class	The teacher asked two students to share with the whole class. These students were already taught how to use gestures when sharing, and they pointed, connected hands, and added in movement as needed to show their thinking.
Reflect	As the period came to an end, the teacher asked the listening students to reflect on what they learned from hearing their peers just share. They were asked to jot down a next step and then act out doing it with their partner. Since they had already gotten over the awkwardness of acting out, and enjoyed it, they did so with ease. This cemented the next step in their bodies and primed them for tomorrow's work.

HOW DO WE BUILD NEW HABITS THAT ALIGN WITH THE BODY AND BRAIN CONNECTION?

Even after reading this book it can be easy to go back to our past ways—to prioritize the brain as the only place where learning happens—because we have been told this story over and over again. Author and embodiment teacher Caldwell (2018) warns us of the four most common traps we fall into:

1. Ignoring our bodies
2. Seeing the body as an object or project
3. Hating the body
4. Making one's body or other people's bodies wrong

If we do this to ourselves, we most certainly will do this to our students, not from any negative intent but because we have been so accustomed to these beliefs.

I suggest we anticipate some struggle with the ideas in this book, especially putting them into practice, and proactively create some routines to help. According to Clear (2018), we can create new habits when we connect our identity to the habit, create systems to support new habits, and focus on small changes that accumulate over time. The following chart lists some ideas for how you might build habits that connect your body and brain so that you can show up as your most effective self and also so that you can offer these same sorts of experiences to your students.

When I am feeling	I can remember to use my body to
Pressure	Stand or sit up tall and take a long exhale breath
Overwhelmed by a challenge	Look at the challenge while standing next to someone that is supportive and trustworthy
Unfocused	Go for a walk in nature or look a picture of natural landscapes
Anxious	Laugh or hold a pencil between my teeth to force a smile
Tension	Do a body scan or tighten and release different parts of my body

(Continued)

(Continued)

When I am feeling	I can remember to use my body to
Confused	Talk to someone while I gesture and move my body freely
Unmotivated	Reach for and pull objects to my body like a book or device to make them feel more attractive
Fatigued	Get rid of clocks and other devices that tell me how long I have been doing something
Distracted	Get rid of background noise, use paper and pen, and read actual print books
Forgetful	Act out what I am trying to remember

There are no simple answers to any of the challenges we educators face today both personally and professionally, but I do know that the body plays a large role and can be a real asset. I've been repatterning my own relationship with my body by simply remembering I have one whenever I can. This means I try to feel the back of my legs while sitting on the chair, feel my feet making contact with the floor, and notice my rib cage's movement when I take a breath. I also allow my body to move. I gesture, I stand up, I make facial expressions, I act with intention. None of these cost money, all are quick, and if I remember to do them, they are all really easy.

In every classroom, every day, students' bodies lead their learning. They literally cannot leave their bodies behind. We teachers can choose to bring more attention and awareness into the ways we can teach students to leverage their body's innate abilities to reduce anxiety, boost engagement, and increase comprehension. I'll remind you of what I said at the start of the book—movement, both big and small, unconscious and conscious, fuels students' learning success.

Appendices

All appendices in this book are available for download from the companion website.
https://companion.corwin.com/courses/bodybrainconnection

APPENDIX A

THE AUTONOMIC LADDER

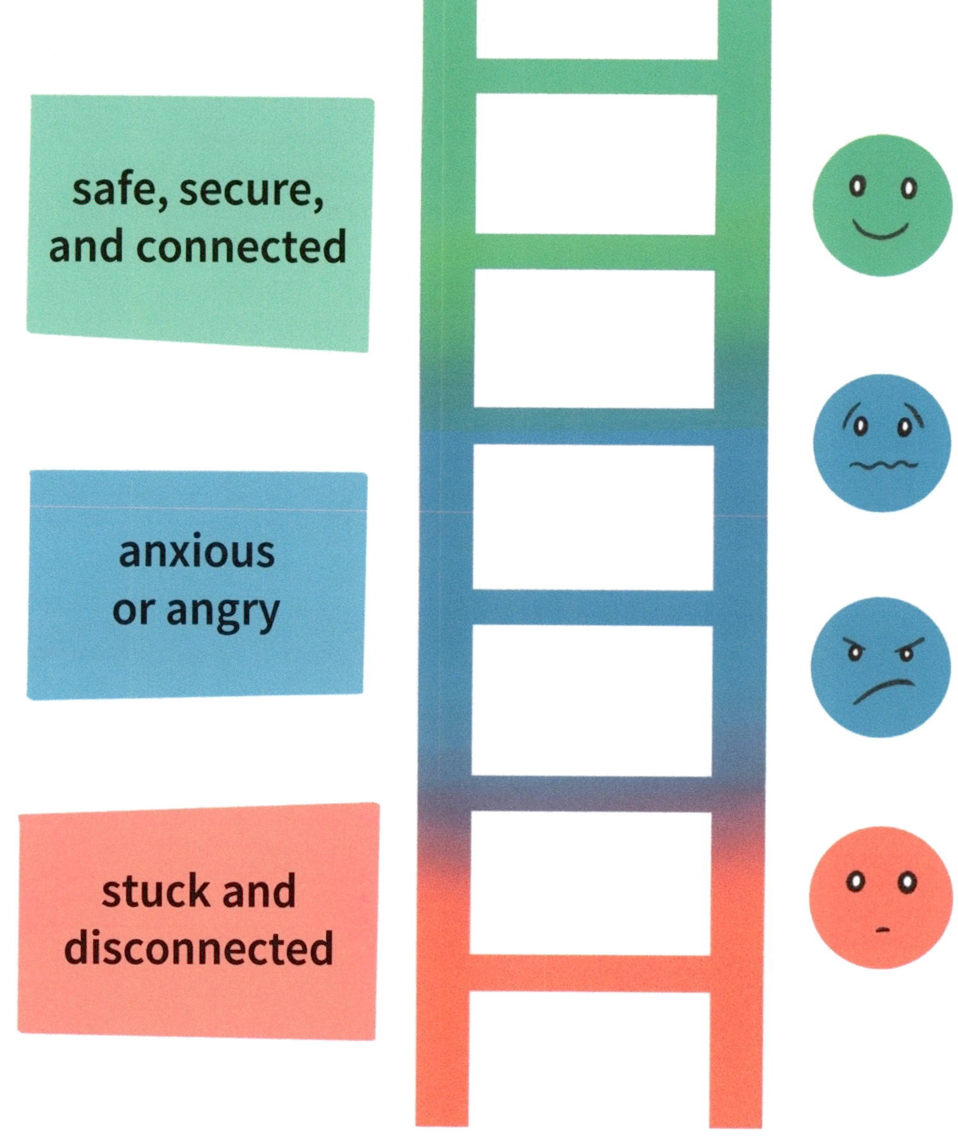

APPENDIX B

SAMPLE LESSON CHART

Tracking Characters' Feeling States in Books

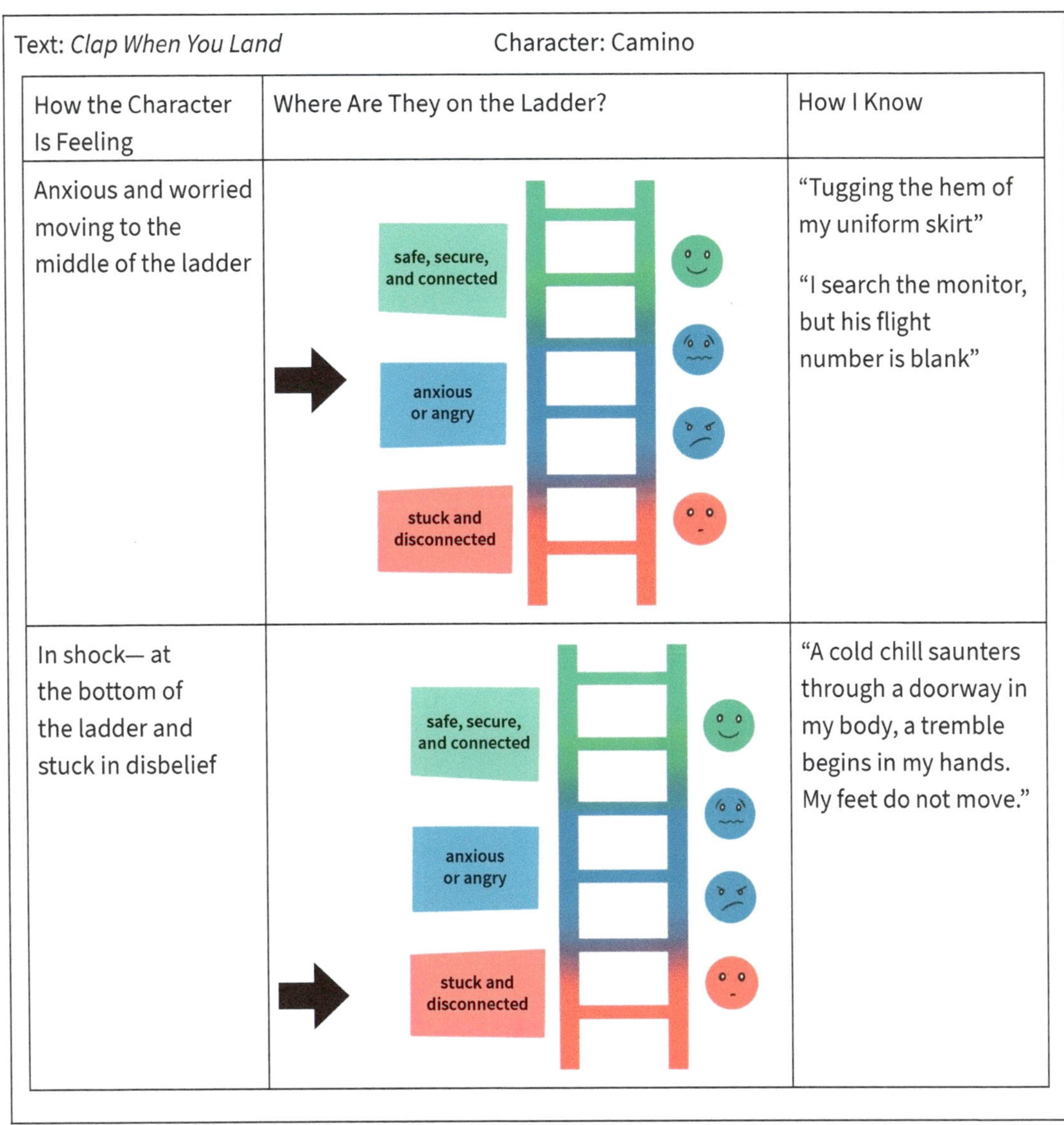

Text: *Clap When You Land* Character: Camino

How the Character Is Feeling	Where Are They on the Ladder?	How I Know
Anxious and worried moving to the middle of the ladder	safe, secure, and connected anxious or angry stuck and disconnected	"Tugging the hem of my uniform skirt" "I search the monitor, but his flight number is blank"
In shock— at the bottom of the ladder and stuck in disbelief	safe, secure, and connected anxious or angry stuck and disconnected	"A cold chill saunters through a doorway in my body, a tremble begins in my hands. My feet do not move."

APPENDIX C

HYPERAROUSAL

- sympathetic nervous system activated
- overwhelmed with emotions
- fight or flight response
- agitated or aggressive, meltdowns, anxiety, hyperactivity and/or hypervigilance

HYPOAROUSAL

- freeze response
- withdrawn/shutdown
- disconnected from the world
- difficulty articulating thoughts

APPENDIX E

WINDOW OF TOLERANCE

- calm and secure
- environment perceived as safe
- social engagement system (ventral vagas) is activated
- control over emotions and thoughts
- optimal zone of arousal

APPENDIX F

THE AGILE APPROACH TO CO-REGULATION

The **AGILE Approach** to co-regulation, developed by the National Institute for Children's Health Quality, offers a framework for caregivers and teachers to help children co-regulate.

- A - **Affect:** How your tone and expressions convey your emotions. In times of stress, is your affect supportive and calm?
- G - **Gesture:** Facial expressions, hand gestures, body movement, posturing, and pacing all reflect your emotions and are felt by a child during your interactions.
- I - **Intonation:** Modulating the tone of your voice helps convey affect and social/emotional meaning. This is "felt" and "understood" long before words. This communication is stronger than words.
- L - **Latency (Wait):** Wait and give the child time to take in your gestures and intonations. Co-regulation requires patience.
- E - **Engagement:** Before you continue, be sure you have engaged the child. The child's facial expressions, sounds, and body language will tell you if they are engaged.

APPENDIX G

BODY SCAN

> A body scan practice is positively and significantly correlated with decreased anxiety and increased non-reactivity. (Carmody & Baer, 2008)

When: at the very start of class or the start of a reading experience, anytime you transition

Time frame: 1–3 minutes

Steps:

1. Tell students they are going to have one minute to set their bodies up for learning.
2. Explain that we are not judging our sensations and our job is to simply notice them. There are no wrong sensations and we are not trying to change anything.
3. Ask students to sit up with their feet planted firmly on the ground. Take an intentional inhale and exhale through the nose. Invite students to close their eyes or bring their gaze down to the floor if they are not comfortable closing their eyes completely.

4. Starting at the feet, invite students to pay attention to what they are feeling in their bodies. Move awareness up the body from the feet, legs, abdomen, chest, arms, shoulders, and face. End by having students feel the contact their feet are making on the ground.
5. Give students a few seconds to sit in silence before ending the experience.

Tips:

- End by asking students to open their eyes and then you can begin teaching. Talking about the sensations may lead to distractions and comparisons and is not necessary.
- Use age-appropriate language so that older students don't feel uncomfortable with the terminology. Yes, there may be giggles at first when you ask them to feel sensations in their bodies, but if you give them a few days of practice the awkwardness should go away. For teens who would balk at anything called a "body scan" you can use more scientific terminology like *interoception*.
- Remind students they can use their breath to relax into any areas that feel tight as they scan. They don't have to do anything, but they can let go of tension.
- After leading students through the scan a few times with success, you can let them do a self-guided body scan. This means instead of telling them what to sense, the students go through the process on their own at their own pace.

The following script is adapted from the Greater Good Science Center (2017).

> Begin by bringing your attention into your body.
>
> You can close your eyes or bring your gaze down to the floor.
>
> Feel the weight of your body on the chair.
>
> Take a few deep and slow breaths.
>
> Notice your feet on the floor. Feel the weight and pressure, vibration, and heat.
>
> Notice your legs against the chair. Feel the pressure, pulsing, heaviness, or lightness.
>
> Notice your back against the chair.
>
> Bring your attention into your stomach. If your stomach is tight, let it soften. Take a breath.
>
> Notice your hands. If your hands are tight, allow them to soften.
>
> Feel any sensation in your arms. Let your shoulders be soft.
>
> Notice your neck and throat. Let them be soft. Relax.
>
> Soften your jaw. Let your face and facial muscles be soft.

APPENDIX H

CALM BREATHING

> "Mindfulness breathing meditation has an impact on reducing stress and anxiety in students." (Komariah et al., 2022)

When: at the very start of class or the start of a reading experience, anytime you transition

Time frame: 1–2 minutes

Steps:

1. Sit up tall with your feet on the floor. Let your arms relax down at your sides.
2. Close your eyes or bring your gaze down to the floor.
3. Slowly breathe in through your nose. Notice your chest filling up with air and your belly expanding.
4. Now slowly breathe out through your nose. Notice your chest emptying and your belly relaxing.

5. Repeat this breathing pattern a few more times.
6. End by returning to your normal breath and noticing how you feel.

Tips:

- You can add a count to the breath, starting with inhaling for two and exhaling for two. Build up to the count of four if students are ready.
- Elongating the exhale for a longer count helps you relax. When the body is holding onto a bit of carbon dioxide it becomes a natural sedative (Han et al., 2023). Invite students who are already comfortable with the breathing exercises to briefly hold their inhalation and then slowly exhale for a few counts longer than they inhaled.
- Make sure that if any student feels dizzy or lightheaded, they stop the exercise and take their time before getting up.
- Always check to make sure students are physically well enough to participate in intentional breathing exercises before inviting them to try.

APPENDIX I

SENSORY NOTICING 5-4-3-2-1

> "This *gesture of awareness* opens us up to the possibility of acting at least a bit more wisely in this world." (Kabat-Zinn, 2021)

When: at the very start of class or the start of a reading experience, anytime you transition

Time frame: 1–2 minutes

Steps:

1. Acknowledge FIVE things you see around you. It could be a chart, a spot on the wall, your teacher's earrings, etc.
2. Acknowledge FOUR things you can touch around you. It could be the metal leg on your chair, the texture of your sweater, or the ground under your feet, etc.

3. Acknowledge THREE things you hear outside your body. This could be students talking in the hallway, a bird chirping outside, yourself tapping your pencil on the desk, etc.
4. Acknowledge TWO things you can smell. This could be the pencil shavings, the lotion on your hands, or someone's rotten apple peel in the garbage, etc.
5. Acknowledge ONE thing you can taste. What does the inside of your mouth taste like? This could be gum, peanut butter from your lunch, or staleness from thirst, etc.

Tips:

- You don't always have to do all five steps. Just taking a moment to have a sensory experience brings us out of our thoughts and into our bodies and environment.
- If students enjoy this practice, try bringing in a candle or playing soft music to include a few more sensory experiences. Just be aware that some scents and sounds are too strong for students, so err on the side of subtle.
- The listening sensory experience on its own can be helpful to create calm in the classroom. Dim the lights, allow students to put their heads down, and then guide them to listen for sounds. They can move from sounds very close to them and try to move their sense of sound out more to the classroom, hallway, outside, etc. How far can they hear?

APPENDIX J

VISUALIZING PERSONAL POWER

> "When we feel personally powerful, we not only show up, but we show up as both strong and generous, as both confident and kind." (Cuddy, 2015)

When: at the very start of class or the start of a reading experience, anytime you transition

Time frame: 30 seconds to 1 minute

Steps:

1. Sit in a comfortable position and close your eyes.
2. Think of a time in your life when you felt personally powerful.
3. Picture the moment. Make a clear movie in your mind of what you were doing and how you felt.
4. Take in that feeling of personal power.

Tips:

- Dr. Amy Cuddy found that a sense of personal power is different from social power. Social power is the ability to control the actions of others, and personal power is our ability to control our own states and actions. This practice is focused on personal power, so make sure students understand the difference.
- When visualizing and feeling into our own personal power, we are priming ourselves to feel more personally powerful and confident for what's coming next. In this way we set ourselves up to feel ready for the next challenge, like reading a new book or learning a new strategy.
- The moment we are picturing does not have to be connected to school or reading. It is not about the content of the moment we are visualizing but is about the feeling associated with it.

APPENDIX K

LAUGHTER YOGA

> "Scientific studies have shown that there is an increase in serotonin and dopamine with laughter yoga." (Laughteryoga.org)

When: at the end of class or reading time, anytime you transition, when students are feeling anxious and need a fresh start to relieve tension

Time frame: 30 seconds to 1 minute

Steps:

1. Stand up and spread out.
2. Begin by clapping rhythmically 1-2, 1-2-3.
3. Add in the sounds "ho-ho, ha-ha-ha" as you clap.
4. Pick up the pace as you go.
5. Drop the clapping and just make the sounds "ho-ho, ha-ha-ha." Possibly add in other gestures like hands up and down.
6. Let yourself smile, move, make eye contact, and connect with one another.

7. A more spontaneous laughter will likely occur. Let that happen.
8. End with a closing routine, such as getting quieter with our voices and doing a long exhalation, before sitting back down.

Tips:

- According to Langer (2024), joy is a way to create regulation in our bodies. When students are joyfully laughing, they are not just reducing anxiety but also creating regulated nervous systems. If students are feeling grumpy, discouraged, and anxious, consider a laughter yoga exercise. Or be proactive and start with one before the period begins.
- Laughing releases endorphins and "happy" hormones like dopamine and serotonin. The release of these hormones is a safe way to help students regulate. And by doing the laughter together you are co-regulating off of one another. If you have a particularly silly class, you can harness their need for laughter with an intentional exercise.
- Don't assume students (of any age) will know how to transition from laughter yoga to the next activity. For this reason, choose laughter yoga after reading as a way to recharge and begin the next learning experience. Teach them how to end the laughing session with a routine that clearly shows you are moving on to the next part of the day. Some ideas for endings include high five a neighbor, sit and feel, or big exhale and jump. After the final action students can practice sitting and being ready to learn again.

SOME VARIATIONS OF LAUGHTER YOGA (KANIGEL, 2021)

Lion laughter: Stick out your tongue, open your eyes wide, and stretch your hands out like claws while laughing.

Humming laughter: Laugh with the mouth closed and hum.

Silent laughter: Open your mouth wide and laugh without making a sound.

Gradient laughter: Start by smiling and then slowly begin to chuckle softly. Increase the intensity of the laugh until you've achieved a hearty laugh. Then gradually bring the laugh down to a smile again. Bonus: this can be an opportunity to teach some vocabulary words if you put the words up on the board as you guide students through the gradient.

Smile	Chuckle	Giggle	Guffaw	Roar

APPENDIX L

WAYS TO BE A SUPPORTIVE PARTNER

- Smile.
- Lean in.
- Nod your head.
- Use positive language such as "I believe you can do it."
- Give them space to do the work themselves.
- Mirror back what you are seeing them do to honor their efforts.

APPENDIX M

SAMPLE LESSON

Shifting the Sequence With Text Difficulty

This set of lessons is focused on the essential questions	The students were asked to do the following:
• Why is connection important? • How does it feel to be connected to others? • How do members of a community form connections?	**1.** First read, to determine what it is literally about. **2.** Second read, focus on the overall messages of the text along with the tone. **3.** Third read, notice the author's choices and how they crafted the messages and tone.

Lesson Sequence

1. The students considered the same essential questions and were asked to use the same close reading process across all three texts. The texts themselves moved from most difficult to least challenging because of what they ask readers to do.
2. The first text has audio but no visuals and many literary devices to interpret. The second text has visuals and audio and mostly relies on metaphors the reader must interpret. The third text is a picture book that has a story structure, colloquial language, and dialogue and plot that are used to interpret the messages.
3. There will be some students (likely outliers) who find the poem (the first text) easier to understand than the picture book (the third text) because they are avid poetry readers, but most students will find the level of difficulty decrease as they move their way through the text set. By working through the most difficult text first, students are not yet fatigued and feeling more confident to keep reading the others.
4. After reading all three texts, students would go back to the essential questions and either write or discuss or both. They will be asked to synthesize ideas and examples from across the texts.

Text	Description
Read and listen to the audio recording of *Remember,* by Joy Harjo (poem).	Poem is full of imagery. Author speaks directly to the reader. Text uses many literary devices the reader must interpret.
Watch the music video of the song *Connection,* by One Republic with the lyrics in front of you.	Visuals from the video help with visualizing. Hearing the melody and pace makes the tone more clear. Metaphors need to be interpreted to understand the messages.
Read the picture book *Carl and the Meaning of Life,* by Deborah Freedman.	Story is direct and linear. Illustrations match what is happening on the page. Dialogue is used to develop the message of the book.

APPENDIX N

MINDFUL READERS CHART

Notice what they do as they read.	"First I . . . then I . . ."
Notice their thinking as they read.	"I'm wondering about . . ."
Notice their feelings as they read.	"I am feeling . . ."
Notice changes.	"This changed when . . ."
Notice differences between characters/topics.	"These are different because . . ."
Notice differences between perspectives.	"I see it like this… and my partner sees it like . . ."

APPENDIX O

COMPREHENSION MANIPULATIVES

Manipulative	How Students and Writers Might Use Them
Play dough	Create models, artifacts, and scenes Make comparisons of size, shape, and distance of objects created Represent pressure, tension, and experience sensory input that matches relationships
Sticky notes (variety of sizes and shapes)	Sequence events by using each sticky to represent an event Organize information into categories with one piece of information per sticky
Blocks	Build ideas by stacking blocks to represent each idea Construct settings that character manipulatives can move within
Figurines	Act out character movements Represent character interactions and relationships Role play scenes
Legos	Construct models Show connections between concepts and ideas with different brick colors, sizes, and shapes Make comparisons with each brick representing one unit/idea/concept
Popsicle stick	Keep track of quantities Use them as pointers Build bridges between other manipulatives
Paper clips	Track quantities Build connections Use them as props when figurines reenact scenes

APPENDIX P

TYPES OF MOVEMENT SUMMARY CHART

Type of Movement	Meaning	Example
Matching Movement	When the movement directly matches the words	Acting like a bunny hopping while reading about a bunny hopping
Goal-Directed Movement	When the movement does not directly match the words but is connected by a goal the words convey	Inferring the character's motivation and making a facial expression and body movement to show what they want (even though those actions are not described in the text)
Experience Movement	When movement introduces us to an abstract concept through a bodily experience	Understanding character relationships by tapping into your feeling of connection and disconnection
Stepping in Movement	When you imagine yourself in the text and move as if you are the topic being read about	Reading about how the water cycle works by acting as if you are a water molecule and imaging the journey of movement you would take
Comparison Movement	When you use movement to understand language by the feeling the movement brings	When reading about a character as "a force of nature," using the feeling of natural forces like large wind gusts to get an understanding of what the character was like—the feeling of the movement the language implies

APPENDIX Q

TYPES OF GESTURE SUMMARY CHART

Type	Description	Example
Iconic	Used to depict movement, action, and shape	Moving arms in running motion like the character
Metaphorical	Used to depict abstract concepts	Moving hand from left to right to represent the passage of time when retelling
Deictic	Pointing gestures	Pointing at a picture of a character on the page
Emblem	Used in place of a word	Thumbs-up sign to signal the word *OK* during a book club conversation
Pragmatic	Communicate interactions	Shrugging shoulders to show lack of interest or uncertainty when asked a question
Beat	Hand moves up and down creating a sort of rhythm	Pumping a fist up and down to emphasize points and draw attention when in a debate

APPENDIX R

QUICK FORMATIVE ASSESSMENT TOOL FOR CAPTURING UNDERSTANDING

Student ______________________ Focus ______________________

What I See	Evidence	What It Might Mean
Gesture-Speech Match Correct Understanding		Student understands and does not need instruction
Gesture-Speech Match Incorrect Understanding		Student does not yet understand and may need more time and experience
Gesture-Speech Mismatch		Student is moving toward understanding and is ready for instruction

Instructional Next Steps:

APPENDIX S

HOW TO USE GESTURES TO DEVELOP UNDERSTANDING

Use Gestures to Understand When	Try Out	How a Listener Can Help
You are confused.	Talk while using gestures and just let your hands move a lot. Allow ideas to flow through your hands. Don't worry about having it all make sense yet.	Have a listener be a mirror and share what they heard AND saw when you were talking.
You want to remember.	Use your hands to offload information by using gestures to hold the information in a representational way for you.	Take notes on what you say and use them to help create a study guide.
You have partial understanding.	Explain what you do know and then purposefully gesture about what you don't yet understand. Allow your hands to show the confusion.	Have a listener focus on the confusion and explain what they saw. Maybe they can pick up on some nuances of understanding you are not yet consciously aware of.
You feel like you understand but don't have the words yet to explain it.	Use gestures to show what you know and let the words follow. Don't pay as much attention to the words yet and let the gesture take the place of words you don't yet have. Gestures can prime your brain for the words. You may be surprised that the words follow the gesture.	Have a listener name back and describe what they saw you gesture. Maybe they can help put words to the ideas you have, or they can simply listen as the words follow the gesture.

APPENDIX T

TEACHER GESTURES FOR MODELING SKILLS

Skills	When You Model and Say	Try These Gestures
Inferring	The character is feeling  . . .	Point to your facial expression, which matches the feeling. Make an emoji symbol with your hands and body (e.g., heart, point to wide eyes, shrug shoulders up).
Sequencing	First, then, next  . . .	Put up a finger as you say each sequence word like you are counting. Move your hand farther away from your body each time you say a new event to show them happening later in time.
Predicting	Because I already know ___, I think ___ will happen next. 	Point to head when you say, "I already know," and then point away from you to show prediction as you unfold your arm.

(Continued)

(Continued)

Synthesizing	If I put this detail and this detail together, it makes me think of this bigger idea that . . . 	Put up one fist for each idea and then clasp the hands together as you say the bigger idea that connects them.
Determining Importance	This detail is sort of small and not that important, but this one is really important because . . . 	Make a tiny pinching hand for a small detail and then expand your hand wide for the important detail (can scrunch and open eyes along with this too).
Envisioning	When I read this, I pictured . . . 	Point to your head as you close your eyes and describe the movie in your mind.

APPENDIX U

WAYS TO TAKE NOTES

1. Get out a notebook and pen.

2. Remind yourself what the focus of the reading is. Jot the focus on the top of the page.

3. As you read, notice when a part of the text matches your focus for reading.

4. Ask yourself, "What does this mean?

5. Think about HOW this information fits with the larger topic/focus.

6. Jot down the page number and use your own words to capture what it says, what it means, and how it connects. Use words, sketches, tables, shapes, or symbols to help you remember your thinking.

APPENDIX V

CLASSROOM MATERIALS

Materials	Why They Are Helpful
Bins with handles	Organize materials so that students experience the flexion/pulling movement that can lead to more positive feelings
Charts for students	Support student reflection and application of strategies you taught
Earbuds/headphones/speakers	Listen to music before work to create motivation and arousal
Comprehension manipulatives (see page 128)	Allows and encourages students to incorporate movement into learning experiences in order to deepen understanding
Nature view (or slides)	Reduces stress and increases awe, leads to more focused attention and less impulsivity
Notebooks	Students can take notes by handwriting to develop conceptual understanding
Pens, pencils, highlighters	Students can take notes in the text and develop conceptual understanding
Print texts	Students can have the sensorimotor experience and develop spatial awareness by reading physical texts
Sensory materials (shave cream, sand, bumpy boards)	Practice handwriting and have sensorimotor experiences for foundational skills
Sticky notes	Mark and locate information and help with indexing and creating a cognitive map of a text
Sensory seating and wobble cushions that allow students to move while still sitting	Create opportunities for movement without having to get up and distract others and provide sensory feedback

References

Achor, S. (2018). *Big potential: How transforming the pursuit of success raises our achievement, happiness, and well-being*. Crown Business.

Altamura, L., Vargas, C., & Salmerón, L. (2023). Do new forms of reading pay off? A meta-analysis on the relationship between leisure digital reading habits and text comprehension. *Review of Educational Research*. Advance online publication. https://doi.org/10.3102/00346543231216463

American Psychological Association. (n.d.). *APA dictionary of psychology*. https://dictionary.apa.org/mindfulness

Anderson, S. A., & Fuller, G. B. (2010). Effect of music on reading comprehension of junior high school students. *School Psychology Quarterly*, *25*(3), 178–187.

Annamma, S. A. (2017). *The pedagogy of pathologization*. Routledge.

Atit, K., Miller, D. I., Newcombe, N. S., & Uttal, D. H. (2018). Teachers' spatial skills across disciplines and education levels: Exploring nationally representative data. *Archives of Scientific Psychology*, *6*(1), 130–137.

Baron, N. S. (2015). *Words onscreen: The fate of reading in a digital world*. Oxford University Press.

Barsalou, L. W. (1999). Perceptions of perceptual symbols. *Behavioral and Brain Sciences, 22*(4), 637–660.

Barsalou, L. W. (2008). Cognitive and neural contributions to understanding the conceptual system. *Current Directions in Psychological Science*, *17*(2), 91–95.

Bartolomeo, P. (2002). The relationship between visual perception and visual mental imagery: A reappraisal of the neuropsychological evidence. *Cortex*, *38*, 357–378.

Bartolomeo, P., Bachoud-Lévi, A.-C., Chokron, S., & Degos, J. D. (2002). Visually- and motor-based knowledge of letters: Evidence from a pure alexic patient. *Neuropsychologia, 40*(8), 1363–1371.

Becvar, L. A., Hollan, J., & Hutchins, E. (2005). Hands as molecules: Representational gestures used for developing theory in a scientific laboratory. *Semiotica*, *2005*, 89–112.

Beilock, S. (2015). *How the body knows its mind: The surprising power of the physical environment to influence how you think and feel*. Atria Books.

Beilock, S. L., & Fischer, S. M. (2013, July 17–18). *From cognitive sciences to physics education and back* [Conference session]. Physics Education Research Conference Proceedings, Portland, OR.

Bergen, B. K. (2012). *Louder than words: The new science of how the mind makes meaning.* Basic Books.

Berry, M. S., Repke, M. A., Nickerson, N. P., Conway, L. G., III, Odum, A. L., & Jordan, K. E. (2015). Making time for nature: Visual exposure to natural environments lengthens subjective time perception and reduces impulsivity. *PLOS ONE, 10*(11), Article e0141030.

Biasutti, M. (2011). The student experience of a collaborative e-learning university module. *Computers & Education, 57*(3), 1865–1875.

Bishop, R. S. (1990). Mirrors, windows, and sliding glass doors. *Perspectives: Choosing and Using Books for the Classroom, 6*(3), ix–xi.

Bornemann, B., Herbert, B. M., Mehling, W. E., & Singer, T. (2015). Differential changes in self-reported aspects of interoceptive awareness through three months of contemplative training. *Frontiers in Psychology, 5*, Article 1504.

Bratman, G., Daily, G., Levy, B., & Gross, J. (2015). The benefits of nature experience: Improved affect and cognition. *Landscape and Urban Planning, 138*, 41–50.

Brower, T. (2021). *The secrets to happiness at work*. Sourcebooks.

Brown, K. W., & Ryan, R. M. (2003). The benefits of being present: Mindfulness and its role in psychological well-being. *Journal of Personality and Social Psychology, 84*, 822–848.

Burrow, A. L., Hill, P. L., & Sumner, R. (2016). Leveling mountains: Purpose attenuates links between perceptions of effort and steepness. *Personality and Social Psychology Bulletin, 42*(1), 94–103.

Caldwell, C. (2018). *Bodyfulness: Somatic practices for presence, empowerment, and waking up in this life*. Shambhala.

Cameron, O. G. (2001). Interoception: The inside story—A model for psychosomatic processes. *Psychosomatic Medicine, 63*, 697–710.

Campaign for Trauma-Informed Policy and Practice. (2022, August 31). *Report: Trauma-informed schools*. https://www.ctipp.org/post/report-trauma-informed-schools

Carlson, C., Jacobs, S. A., Perry, M., & Church, R. B. (2014). The effect of gestured instruction on the learning of physical causality problems. *Gesture, 14*(1), 26–45.

Carmody, J., & Baer, R. A. (2008). Relationships between mindfulness practice and levels of mindfulness, medical and psychological symptoms and well-being in a mindfulness-based stress reduction program. *Journal of Behavioral Medicine, 31*(1), 23–33.

Cartwright, K. (2023). *Executive skills and reading comprehension: A guide for educators* (2nd ed.). Guilford Press.

Cho, B. Y., Hwang, H., & Jang, B. G. (2021). Predicting fourth grade digital reading comprehension: A secondary data analysis of (e)PIRLS 2016. *International Journal of Educational Research, 105*, Article 101696.

Chomsky, N. (1965). *Aspects of the theory of syntax.* MIT Press.

Chomsky, N. (1975). *Reflections on language*. Pantheon Books.

Church, R. B., & Goldin-Meadow, S. (1986). The mismatch between gesture and speech as an index of transitional knowledge. *Cognition, 23*(1), 43–71.

Clark, J. M., & Paivio, A. (1991). Dual coding theory and education. *Educational Psychology Review*, *3*(3), 149–210.

Clear, J. (2018). *Atomic habits: An easy & proven way to build good habits and break bad ones.* Avery.

Cook, S. W., & Goldin-Meadow, S. (2006). The role of gesture in learning: Do children use their hands to change their minds? *Journal of Cognition and Development*, *7*(2), 211–232.

Cope, B. (2015). *A pedagogy of multiliteracies.* Palgrave Macmillan.

Coppola, S. (2023). *Literacy for all: A framework for anti-oppressive teaching*. Routledge.

Cowan, N. (2001). The magical number 4 in short-term memory: A reconsideration of mental storage capacity. *Behavioral and Brain Sciences*, *24*(1), 87–185.

Cowan, N. (2014). Working memory underpins cognitive development, learning, and education. *Educational Psychology Review*, *26*(2), 197–223.

Crowder, E. M. (1996). Gestures at work in sense-making science talk. *Journal of the Learning Sciences*, *5*(3), 173–208.

Cuddy, A. (2015). *Presence: Bringing your boldest self to your biggest challenges.* Little, Brown.

Cunningham, A. E., & Stanovich, K. E. (1990). Early spelling acquisition: Writing beats the computer. *Journal of Educational Psychology*, *82*(1), 159–162.

Damasio, A. (2003). The person within. *Nature*, *423*(6937), 227.

Dana, D. (2023). *Polyvagal practices: Anchoring the self in safety*. Norton.

Dargue, N., & Sweller, N. (2020). Learning stories through gesture: Gesture's effects on child and adult narrative comprehension. *Educational Psychology Review*, *32*(1), 249–276.

Dargue, N., Sweller, N., & Jones, M. P. (2019). When our hands help us understand: A meta-analysis into the effects of gesture on comprehension. *Psychological Bulletin*, *145*(8), 765–784.

de Jong, M., Lazar, S. W., Hug, K., Mehling, W. E., Hölzel, B. K., Sack, A. T., Peeters, F., Ashih, H., Mischoulon, D., & Gard, T. (2016). Effects of mindfulness-based cognitive therapy on body awareness in patients with chronic pain and comorbid depression. *Frontiers in Psychology*, *7*, Article 967.

Devereaux, C. (2017). An interview with Dr. Stephen W. Porges. *American Journal of Dance Therapy, 39*, 27–35. https://link.springer.com/article/10.1007/s10465-017-9252-6

Dickinson, D. K., Golinkoff, R. M., & Hirsh-Pasek, K. (2010). Speaking out for language: Why language is central to reading development. *Educational Researcher*, *39*(4), 305–310.

Dillon, A. (1992). Reading from paper versus screens: A critical review of the empirical literature. *Ergonomics*, *35*(10), 1297–1326.

Ditto, B., Eclache, M., & Goldman, N. (2006). Short-term autonomic and cardiovascular effects of mindfulness body scan meditation. *Annals of Behavioral Medicine*, *32*(3), 227–234.

Duke, N. K., & Cartwright, K. B. (2021). The science of reading progresses: Communicating advances beyond the simple view of reading. *Reading Research Quarterly*, *56*(S1), S25–S44.

Engel, A. K., Maye, A., Kurthen, M., & König, P. (2013). Where's the action? The pragmatic turn in cognitive science. *Trends in Cognitive Sciences*, *17*(5), 202–209.

Erwin, E. J., & Robinson, K. R. (2016). The joy of being: Making way for young children's natural mindfulness. *Early Child Development and Care*, *186*(2), 268–286.

Farb, N. A., Segal, Z. V., Mayberg, H., Bean, J., McKeon, D., Fatima, Z., & Anderson, A. K. (2007). Attending to the present: Mindfulness meditation reveals distinct neural modes of self-reference. *Social Cognitive and Affective Neuroscience*, *2*(4), 313–322.

Fischer, M. A., & Shrout, P. (2006). Children's liking of landscape paintings as a function of their perceptions of prospect, refuge, and hazard. *Environment and Behavior*, *38*, 373–393.

Fissler, M., Winnebeck, E., Schroeter, T., Gummersbach, M., Huntenburg, J. M., Gaertner, M., & Barnhofer, T. (2016). An investigation of the effects of brief mindfulness training on self-reported interoceptive awareness, the ability to decenter, and their role in the reduction of depressive symptoms. *Mindfulness*, *7*, 1170–1181.

Flanigan, A. E., Wheeler, J., Colliot, T., Lu, J., & Kiewra, K. A. (2024). Typed versus handwritten lecture notes and college student achievement: A meta-analysis. *Educational Psychology Review*, *36*(3), Article 78.

Fodor, J. A., Bever, T. G., & Garrett, M. F. (1974). *The psychology of language: An introduction to psycholinguistics and generative grammar*. McGraw-Hill.

Gleaves, L. (2023). *Anxiety through the lens of polyvagal theory*. https://www.counselling-directory.org.uk/articles/anxiety-through-the-lens-of-polyvagal-theory

Glenberg, A. M., & Gallese, V. (2012). Action-based language: A theory of language acquisition, comprehension, and production. *Cortex*, *48*(7), 905–922.

Glenberg, A. M., Gutierrez, T., Levin, J. R., Japuntich, S., & Kaschak, M. P. (2004). Activity and imagined activity can enhance young children's reading comprehension. *Journal of Educational Psychology*, *96*, 424–436.

Glenberg, A. M., & Kaschak, M. P. (2002). Grounding language in action. *Psychonomic Bulletin & Review*, *9*(3), 558–565.

Glenberg, A. M., & Robertson, D. A. (2000). Symbol grounding and meaning: A comparison of high-dimensional and embodied theories of meaning. *Journal of Memory and Language*, *43*(3), 379–401.

Goetz, T., & Hall, N. C. (2013). Emotion and achievement in the classroom. In J. Hattie & E. M. Anderman (Eds.), *International guide to student achievement* (pp. 192–195). Routledge.

Goldberg, G. (2018). *Teach like yourself*. Corwin Press.

Goldin-Meadow, S. (2005). *Hearing gesture: How our hands help us think*. Belknap Press of Harvard University Press.

Goldin-Meadow, S., Nusbaum, H., Kelly, S. D., & Wagner, S. (2001). Explaining math: Gesturing lightens the load. *Psychological Science*, *12*(6), 516–522.

Goodwin, A. P., Cho, S., Reynolds, D., Brady, K., & Salas, J. (2020). Digital versus paper reading processes and links to comprehension for middle school students. *American Educational Research Journal*, *57*(4), 1837–1867.

Gough, P. B., & Tunmer, W. E. (1986). Decoding, reading, and reading disability. *Remedial and Special Education*, *7*, 6–10.

Greater Good Science Center. (n.d.). *Body scan meditation*. University of California, Berkeley. https://ggia.berkeley.edu/practice/body_scan_meditation

Griffin, J. B., Jr. (1990). Anxiety. In H. K. Walker, W. D. Hall, & J. W. Hurst (Eds.), *Clinical methods: The history, physical, and laboratory examinations* (3rd ed.). Butterworths. https://www.ncbi.nlm.nih.gov/books/NBK315/

Haidt, J. (2012). *The righteous mind: Why good people are divided by politics and religion.* Pantheon Books.

Han, H., Kim, D., Kim, J. S., Kwac, L. K., Hyeon, J., & Oh, J. (2023). A novel sleep aid device to reduce sleep latency using air-CO_2 mixed gas. *Frontiers in Neurology*, *14*, Article 1163904.

Heuer, F., & Reisberg, D. (2014). Emotion, arousal and memory for detail. In S.-A. Christianson (Ed.), *The handbook of emotion and memory: Research and theory* (pp. 151–180). Psychology Press.

Hinton, S. E. (1967). *The outsiders*. Viking Press.

Hölzel, B. K., Carmody, J., Vangel, M., Congleton, C., Yerramsetti, S. M., Gard, T., & Lazar, S. W. (2011). Mindfulness practice leads to increases in regional brain gray matter density. *Psychiatry Research*, *191*(1), 36–43.

Hou, J., Rashid, J., & Lee, K. M. (2017). Cognitive map or medium materiality? Reading on paper and screen. *Computers in Human Behavior*, *67*, 84–94.

Husain, G., Thompson, W. F., & Schellenberg, E. G. (2002). Effects of musical tempo and mode on arousal, mood, and spatial abilities. *Music Perception: An Interdisciplinary Journal*, *20*(2), 151–171.

Isen, A. M. (2002). A role for neuropsychology in understanding the facilitating influence of positive affect on social behavior and cognitive processes. In C. R. Snyder & S. J. Lopez (Eds.), *Handbook of positive psychology* (pp. 528–540). Oxford University Press.

Jabr, F. (2013). Why the brain prefers paper. *Scientific American, 309*(5), 48–53.

Jaffe, E. (2004, July 27). Giving students a hand. *Observer*. Association for Psychological Science. https://www.psychologicalscience.org/observer/giving-students-a-hand-william-james-lecturer-goldin-meadow-shows-the-importance-of-gesture-in-teaching

James, K. H. (2017). The importance of handwriting experience on the development of the literate brain. *Current Directions in Psychological Science*, *26*(6), 502–508.

Jiang, B., Chang, C. Y., & Sullivan, W. C. (2014). A dose of nature: Tree cover, stress reduction, and gender differences. *Landscape and Urban Planning*, *132*, 26–36.

Johnston, P. H. (2024). *Choice words: How our language affects children's learning* (2nd ed.). Routledge.

Joye, Y., Steg, L., Unal, A. B., & Pals, R. (2015). When complex is easy on the mind: Internal repetition of visual information in complex objects is a source of perceptual fluency. *Journal of Experimental Psychology: Human Perception and Performance*, *42*(1), 103–114.

Juslin, P. N., & O'Neill, S. A. (2001). Psychological perspectives on music and emotion. In P. N. Juslin & J. A. Sloboda (Eds.), *Music and emotion: Theory and research* (pp. 71–104). Oxford University Press.

Juslin, P. N., & Sloboda, J. A. (2001). *Music and emotion: Theory and research*. Oxford University Press.

Kabat-Zinn, J. (2021). The invitation within the cultivation of mindfulness. *Mindfulness, 12*(4), 1034–1037.

Kämpfe, J., Sedlmeier, P., & Renkewitz, F. (2011). The impact of background music on adult listener: A meta-analysis. *Psychology of Music, 39*, 424–448.

Kang, M. J., Hsu, M., Krajbich, I. M., Loewenstein, G., McClure, S. M., Wang, J. T. Y., & Camerer, C. F. (2009). The wick in the candle of learning: Epistemic curiosity activates reward circuitry and enhances memory. *Psychological Science, 20*, 963–973.

Kanigel, R. (2021). *How laughter yoga heals, plus 6 fun exercises to try*. https://www.yogajournal.com/lifestyle/laughter-cure/

Kaplan, S., & Berman, M. G. (2010). Directed attention as a common resource for executive functioning and self-regulation. *Perspectives on Psychological Science, 5*(1), 43–57.

Katz, I., & Assor, A. (2006). When choice motivates and when it does not. *Educational Psychology Review, 19*, 429–442.

Keehner, M., & Gathercole, S. E. (2007). Cognitive adaptations arising from nonnative experience of sign language in hearing adults. *Memory & Cognition, 35*(4), 752–761.

Keier, K. (2012, July 26). Be the character. *Catching Readers Before They Fall*. https://catchingreaders.com/tag/peter-johnston

Kelly, S. D., Ward, S., Creigh, P., & Bartolotti, J. (2007). An intentional stance modulates the integration of gesture and speech during comprehension. *Brain and Language, 101*, 222–233.

Kerr, R., & Booth, B. (1978). Specific and varied practice of motor skill. *Perceptual and Motor Skills, 46*(2), 395-401.

Kiefer, S. M., Alley, K. M., & Ellerbrock, C. R. (2015). Teacher and peer support for young adolescents' motivation, engagement, and school belonging. *RMLE Online, 38*, 1–18.

Kinney, J. (2007). *Diary of a wimpy kid: Greg Heffley's journal*. Amulet Books.

Kita, S., & Emmorey, K. (2023). Gesture links language and cognition for spoken and signed languages. *Nature Reviews Psychology, 2*, 407–420.

Komariah, M., Ibrahim, K., Pahria, T., Rahayuwati, L., & Somantri, I. (2022). Effect of mindfulness breathing meditation on depression, anxiety, and stress: A randomized controlled trial among university students. *Healthcare (Basel, Switzerland), 11*(1), 26.

Krueger, J. (2024). Affordances and spatial agency in psychopathology. *Philosophical Psychology, 37*(7), 1828–1857.

Kuo, M., Browning, M. H. E. M., & Penner, M. L. (2018). Do lessons in nature boost subsequent classroom engagement? Refueling students in flight. *Frontier Psychology, 8*, Article 253.

Lahoti, A. (2023, February 28). Dopamine and serotonin: Our own happy chemicals. *700 Children's*. https://www.nationwidechildrens.org/family-resources-education/700childrens/2023/02/dopamine-and-serotonin

Lakey, C., Kernis, M., Heppner, W., & Lance, C. (2008). Individual differences in authenticity and mindfulness as predictors of verbal defensiveness. *Journal of Research in Personality, 42*, 230–238.

Lakoff, G., & Johnson, M. (1980). *Metaphors we live by*. University of Chicago Press.

Langer, E. J. (2009). *Counterclockwise: Mindful health and the power of possibility*. Ballantine Books.

Langer, E. J. (2024). *The mindful body*. Penguin Random House.

Langer, E. J., & Rodin, J. (1976). The effects of choice and enhanced personal responsibility for the aged: A field experiment in an institutional setting. *Journal of Personality and Social Psychology, 34*(2), 191–198.

Lehmann, J. A. M., & Seufert, T. (2017). The influence of background music on learning in the light of different theoretical perspectives and the role of working memory capacity. *Frontiers in Psychology, 8*, Article 1902.

Leung, A. K.-y., Kim, S., Polman, E., Ong, L. S., Qiu, L., Goncalo, J. A., & Sanchez-Burks, J. (2012). Embodied metaphors and creative "acts." *Psychological Science, 23*, 502–509.

Li, J. X., & James, K. H. (2016). Handwriting generates variable visual output to facilitate symbol learning. *Journal of Experimental Psychology: General, 145*(3), 298–313.

Li, L.-Y., Chen, G.-D., & Yang, S.-J. (2013). Construction of cognitive maps to improve e-book reading and navigation. *Computers & Education, 60*, 32–39.

Link, T., Nuerk, H.-C., & Moeller K. (2014). On the relation between the mental number line and arithmetic competencies. *Quarterly Journal of Experimental Psychology, 67*(8), 1597–1613.

Longcamp, M., Boucard, C., Gilhodes, J.-C., & Velay, J.-L. (2006). Remembering the orientation of newly learned characters depends on the associated writing knowledge: A comparison between handwriting and typing. *Human Movement Science, 25*, 646–656.

Longcamp, M., Zerbato-Poudou, M.-T., & Velay, J.-L. (2005). The influence of writing practice on letter recognition in preschool children: A comparison between handwriting and typing. *Acta Psychologica, 119*, 67–79.

Love, B. L. (2023). *Punished for dreaming: How school reform harms Black children and how we heal*. St. Martin's Press.

Lymeus, F., Ahrling, M., Apelman, J., Florin, C. M., Nilsson, C., Vincenti, J., Zetterberg, A., Lindberg, P., & Hartig, T. (2020). Mindfulness-Based Restoration Skills Training (ReST) in a natural setting compared to conventional mindfulness training: Psychological functioning after a five-week course. *Frontiers in Psychology, 11*, Article 1560.

Mahon, B. Z., & Hickok, G. (2016). Arguments about the nature of concepts: Symbols, embodiment, and beyond. *Psychonomic Bulletin & Review, 23*(4), 941–958.

Marley, S., Levin, J., & Glenberg, A. (2010). What cognitive benefits does an activity-based reading strategy afford young Native American readers? *Journal of Experimental Education, 78*, 395–417.

Martin, D. J., Garske, J. P., & Davis, M. K. (2000). Relation of the therapeutic alliance with outcome and other variables: A meta-analytic review. *Journal of Consulting and Clinical Psychology, 68*(3), 438–450.

Mastrothanasis, K., Kladaki, M., & Andreou, A. (2023). A systematic review and meta-analysis of the readers' theatre impact on the development of reading skills. *International Journal of Educational Research Open*, *4*, Article 100243.

Mayer, R. E. (2001). *Multimedia learning.* Cambridge University Press.

Mayer, R. E. (2021). Evidence-based principles for how to design effective instructional videos. *Journal of Applied Research in Memory and Cognition*, *10*(2), 229–240.

McDonald, S., & Stevenson, R. J. (1998). Navigation in hyperspace: An evaluation of the effects of navigational tools and subject matter expertise on browsing and information retrieval in hypertext. *Interacting with Computers*, *10*(2), 129–142.

McNeil, N. M., Alibali, M. W., & Evans, J. L. (2000). The role of gesture in children's comprehension of spoken language: Now they need it, now they don't. *Journal of Nonverbal Behavior*, *24*(2), 131–150.

Miller, G. A. (1994). The magical number seven, plus or minus two: Some limits on our capacity for processing information. *Psychological Review*, *101*, 343–352.

Morgan, P., & Abrahamson, D. (2018). Applying contemplative practices to the educational design of mathematics content: Report from a pioneering workshop. *Journal of Contemplative Inquiry*, *5*(1), Article 10.

Mueller, P. A., & Oppenheimer, D. M. (2014). The pen is mightier than the keyboard. *Psychological Science*, *25*(6), 1159–1168.

National Center for Education Statistics. (2024). *English learners in public schools.* U.S. Department of Education, Institute of Education Sciences. https://nces.ed.gov/programs/coe/indicator/cgf/english-learners

National Institute for Children's Health Quality. (2019, April 24). Children's social and emotional development starts with co-regulation. *nichQ.* https://nichq.org/insight/childrens-social-and-emotional-development-starts-co-regulation

Niedenthal, P. M. (2007). Embodying emotion. *Science*, *316*(5827), 1002–1005.

Niedenthal, P. M., Mermillod, M., Maringer, M., & Hess, U. (2010). The simulation of smiles (SIMS) model: Embodied simulation and the meaning of facial expression. *Behavioral and Brain Sciences*, *33*(6), 417–433.

Noice, H., & Noice, T. (2001). Learning dialogue with and without movement. *Memory & Cognition*, *29*(6), 820–827.

Noice, H., & Noice, T. (2007). The non-literal enactment effect: Filling in the blanks. *Discourse Processes, 44*, 73–89.

Noice, H., Noice, T., & Kennedy, C. (2000). Effects of enactment by professional actors at encoding and retrieval. *Memory*, *8*(6), 353–363.

Office of English Language Acquisition. (n.d.). *Benefits of multilingualism.* https://ncela.ed.gov/sites/default/files/legacy/files/announcements/20200805-NCELAInfographic-508.pdf

O'Hara, K., & Sellen, A. (1997, March 22–27). *A comparison of reading paper and on-line documents* [Conference session]. Proceedings of the ACM SIGCHI Conference on Human Factors in Computing Systems, Atlanta, GA (pp. 335–342). ACM.

Oppezzo, M., & Schwartz, D. L. (2014). Give your ideas some legs: The positive effect of walking on creative thinking. *Journal of Experimental Psychology: Learning, Memory, and Cognition, 40*(4), 1142–1152.

Ose Askvik, E., van der Weel, F. R., & van der Meer, A. L. H. (2020). The importance of cursive handwriting over typewriting for learning in the classroom: A high-density EEG study of 12-year-old children and young adults. *Frontiers in Psychology, 11*, Article 550116.

Paris, D. (2012). Culturally sustaining pedagogy: A needed change in stance, terminology, and practice. *Educational Researcher, 41*(3), 93–97. https://doi.org/10.3102/0013189X12441244

Paul, A. M. (2021). *The extended mind: The power of thinking outside the brain*. Houghton Mufflin Harcourt.

Payne, S. J., & Reader, W. R. (2006). Constructing structure maps of multiple on-line texts. *International Journal of Human-Computer Studies, 64*(5), 461–474.

Pekrun, R. (2006). The control-value theory of achievement emotions: Assumptions, corollaries, and implications for educational research and practice. *Educational Psychology Review, 18*(4), 315–341.

Pekrun, R., Lichtenfeld, S., Marsh, H. W., Murayama, K., & Goetz, T. (2017). Achievement emotions and academic performance: Longitudinal models of reciprocal effects. *Child Development, 88*(5), 1653–1670.

Perham, N., & Currie, H. (2014). Does listening to preferred music improve reading comprehension performance? *Applied Cognitive Psychology, 28*(2), 279–284.

Pine, K. J., Bird, H., & Kirk, E. (2007). The effects of prohibiting gestures on children's lexical retrieval ability. *Developmental Science, 10*(6), 747–754.

Pink, D. H. (2009). *Drive: The surprising truth about what motivates us*. Riverhead Books.

Polyvagal Institute. (n.d.) *What is polyvagal theory?* https://www.polyvagalinstitute.org/whatispolyvagaltheory

Porges S. W. (2009). The polyvagal theory: New insights into adaptive reactions of the autonomic nervous system. *Cleveland Clinic Journal of Medicine, 76*(Suppl 2), S86–S90.

Porges, S. W. (2011). *The polyvagal theory: Neurophysiological foundations of emotions, attachment, communication, and self-regulation*. Norton.

Porges, S. W., Doussard-Roosevelt, J. A., & Maita, A. K. (1994). Vagal tone and the physiological regulation of emotion. *Monographs of the Society for Research in Child Development, 59*(2–3), 167–186, 250–283.

Price, C. (2021). *Power of fun: How to feel alive again.* Dial Press.

Pulvermüller, F. (1999). Words in the brain's language. *Behavioral and Brain Sciences, 22*(2), 253–336.

Pulvermüller, F. (2003). *The neuroscience of language: On brain circuits of words and serial order*. Cambridge University Press.

Rey, G. (2012). A review of research and a meta-analysis of the seductive detail effect. *Educational Research Review, 7*(3), 216–237. https://doi.org/10.1016/j.edurev.2012.05.003

Rock, D. (2014). *Quiet leadership*. HarperCollins.

Roth, M., & Lawless, D. (2002). Science, culture, and the emergence of language. *Science Education*, *86*, 368–385.

Rothkopf, E. Z., & Coatney, R. P. (1974). Effects of readability of context passages on subsequent inspection rates. *Journal of Applied Psychology*, *59*(6), 679–682.

Ryan, R. M., & Deci, E. L. (2000). Self-determination theory and the facilitation of intrinsic motivation, social development, and well-being. *American Psychologist*, *55*, 68–78.

Salamé, P., & Baddeley, A. D. (1989). Effects of background music on phonological short-term memory. *Quarterly Journal of Experimental Psychology A: Human Experimental Psychology*, *41*(1-A), 107–122.

Sanchez, C. A., & Wiley, J. (2006). An examination of the seductive details effect in terms of working memory capacity. *Memory & Cognition*, *34*(2), 344–355.

Scherr, R., Close, H. G., Close, E. W., Flood, V. J., McKagan, S. B., Robertson, A. D., Seeley, L., Wittmann, M. C., & Vokos, S. (2013). Negotiating energy dynamics through embodied action in a materially structured environment. *Physical Review Physics Education Journal, 9*, Article 020105. https://doi.org/10.1103/PhysRevSTPER.9.020105

Schmidt, L. A., & Trainor L. J. (2010). Frontal brain electrical activity (EEG) distinguishes valence and intensity of musical emotions. *Cognitive Emotion*, *15*, 487–500.

Schnall, S., Haidt, J., Clore, G. L., & Jordan, A. H. (2008). Disgust as embodied moral judgment. *Personality and Social Psychology Bulletin*, *34*, Article 1096.

Schneps, M. H., Thomson, J. M., Chen, C., Sonnert, G., & Pomplun, M. (2013). E-readers are more effective than paper for some with dyslexia. *PLOS ONE*, *8*(9), Article e75634.

Seidenberg, M. S. (2017). *Language at the speed of sight: How we read, why so many can't, and what can be done about it*. Basic Books.

Seki, K., Yajima, M., & Sugishita, M. (1995). The efficacy of kinesthetic reading treatment for pure alexia. *Neuropsychologia*, *33*, 595–609.

Serafini, F. (2014). *Reading the visual: An introduction to teaching multimodal literacy*. Teachers College Press.

Shalaby, C. (2017). *Troublemakers: Lessons in freedom from young children at school*. New Press.

Shiota, M., Campos, B., & Keltner, D. (2003). The faces of positive emotion: Prototype displays of awe, amusement, and pride. *Annals of the New York Academy of Sciences*, 1000, 296–299. 10.1196/annals.1280.029

Smoker, T. J., Murphy, C. E., & Rockwell, A. K. (2009). Comparing memory for handwriting versus typing. *Proceedings of the Human Factors and Ergonomics Society Annual Meeting*, *53*, 1744–1747.

Son, J. Y., Ramos, P., DeWolf, M., Loftus, W., & Stigler, J. W. (2018). Exploring the practicing-connections hypothesis: Using gesture to support coordination of ideas in understanding a complex statistical concept. *Cognitive Research: Principles and Implications*, *3*, Article 1.

Sriram, R. (2020, April 13). *The neuroscience behind productive struggle*. Edutopia. https://www.edutopia.org/article/neuroscience-behind-productive-struggle/

Substance Abuse and Mental Health Services Administration. (n.d.). *Child trauma*. https://www.samhsa.gov/child-trauma/understanding-child-trauma

Taylor, S. R. (2018). *The body is not an apology: The power of radical self-love*. Berrett-Koehler.

Turkle, S. (2015). *Reclaiming conversation: The power of talk in a digital age*. Penguin Press.

Tversky, B. (2019). *Mind in motion*. Basic Books.

Urry, H. L., Crittle, C. S., Floerke, V. A., Leonard, M. Z., Perry, C. S., III, Akdilek, N., Albert, E. R., Block, A. J., Bollinger, C. A., Bowers, E. M., Brody, R. S., Burk, K. C., Burnstein, A., Chan, A. K., Chan, P. C., Chang, L. J., Chen, E., Chiarawongse, C. P., Chin, G., . . . Zarrow, J. E. (2021). Don't ditch the laptop just yet: A direct replication of Mueller and Oppenheimer's (2014) study 1 plus mini meta-analyses across similar studies. *Psychological Science*, *32*(3), 326–339.

van der Kolk, B. (2014). *The body keeps the score: Brain, mind, and body in the healing of trauma*. Penguin Books.

van der Wal, A. J., Schade, H. M., Krabbendam, L., & van Vugt, M. (2013). Do natural landscapes reduce future discounting in humans? *Proceedings of The Royal Society Biological Sciences*, *280*, Article 20132295. http://doi.org/10.1098/rspb.2013.2295

van der Weel, F. R., & Van der Meer, A. L. H. (2024). Handwriting but not typewriting leads to widespread brain connectivity: A high-density EEG study with implications for the classroom. *Frontiers in Psychology*, *14*, Article 1219945.

Vinci-Booher, S., Cheng, H., & James, K. H. (2019). An analysis of the brain systems involved with producing letters by hand. *Journal of Cognitive Neuroscience*, *31*(1), 138–154.

Walkington, C., Boncoddo, R., Williams, C., Nathan, M. J., Alibali, M. W., Simon, E., & Pier, E. (2014). Being mathematical relations: Dynamic gestures support mathematical reasoning. In W. Penuel, S. A. Jurow, & K. O'Connor (Eds.), *Learning and becoming in practice: Proceedings of the Eleventh International Conference of the Learning Sciences* (Vol. 1, pp. 479–486). University of Colorado.

Waytz, A., & Mason, M. (2014). Your brain at work. What a new approach to neuroscience can teach us about management. *Harvard Business Review*, *91*, 102–111, 134.

Willems, M. (2017). *Let's go for a drive!* Hyperion.

Wolf, M. (2018). *Reader, come home: The reading brain in a digital world.* HarperCollins.

Yerkes, R. M., & Dodson, J. D. (1908). The relation of strength of stimulus to rapidity of habit-formation. *Journal of Comparative Neurology and Psychology, 18*(5), 459–482. https://doi.org/10.1002/cne.920180503

Zelenski, J. M., Dopko, R., & Capaldi, C. (2015, June). Cooperation is in our nature: Nature exposure may promote cooperative and environmentally sustainable behavior. *Journal of Environmental Psychology, 42*, 24–31.

Zenner, C., Herrnleben-Kurz, S., & Walach, H. (2014). Mindfulness-based interventions in schools—A systematic review and meta-analysis. *Frontiers in Psychology, 5*, Article 603.

Index

Zeitfracht Medien GmbH
Ferdinand-Jühlke-Straße 7
99095 Erfurt, Deutschland
produktsicherheit@kolibri360.de